What Every Woman Should Know About Retirement

What
Every Woman
Should Know
About
Retirement

Edited by
Helen Franks

AGE
Concern

© 1987 Age Concern England
Bernard Sunley House
60 Pitcairn Road
Mitcham, Surrey CR4 3LL

ISBN 0 86242 054 7

Age Concern Editor Lee Bennett

Design and Art Direction Eugenie Dodd

Production Joyce O'Shaughnessy

Typeset from disc by Parchment
(Oxford) Ltd.

Printed and bound in Great Britain by
Biddles Ltd., Guildford, Surrey

Contents

Introduction Helen Franks

If you are reading this book, then you are interested in retirement, probably your own or that of someone you are close to. You may be looking forward to this new direction in your life, or wishing it would go away. The idea of retirement means freedom and relief to some people, restriction and isolation to others. And because most of us fear the unknown, at least a little bit, most of us are likely to feel a mixture – both happy anticipation and apprehension.

Retirement for women may feel less drastic a change than it often does for men, who base so much of their identity on their work, but it is also more complex, affecting many parts of our lives. For instance, women take on the emotional welfare in relationships, so we are likely to feel more acutely the effects of two retirements – our partner's as well as our own. One of the things this book examines is the impact of retirement on marriage, his and hers, from a woman's point of view. Even a woman who does not have an outside job may have an outside life which she wishes to continue when her partner retires. How does she retain her autonomy and independence without withdrawing her support?

Many women face retirement alone, and then the possible prospects are very different. They may be widowed, or, increasingly, divorced, perhaps having to leave a busy and engrossing job, after a lifetime working amongst people. For some, this spells liberation. Retiring alone can mean time at last to pursue interests that have been neglected for years. It can mean time to spend with grandchildren and family, time to travel or to stay quietly at home.

But, for others, when the lifeline of a job has gone, the prospect can look uncertain. Will there be loneliness, will it be difficult to find a new identity? As this book shows, loneliness can be a state of mind, and being alone or seeking outside contacts can be a matter of choice. Retirement for women, perhaps even more than for men, provides opportunities to explore a new identity. The many organisations listed in the Directory on page 143 offer scope for anyone wanting to expand her horizons.

By this time of life, most women have already been through several changes. We have outlived our role as mothers of small children, and may find ourselves as grandmothers, with all the joy and none of the responsibilities, and what could be better than that?

But as a our parents age, we are no longer daughters, the ones who were traditionally dependent. We become the carers, they the dependants. It is a role women find given to them time and time again, till they become too old to cope with it. There are not only elderly parents to care for. The handicapped child at a special school until 16 or 18 can then become the handicapped adult dependent on a mother because there is no institution available. Even the divorcing daughter might throw herself and her children on her mother's doorstep for a time. It has been estimated that one in four women between the ages of 50 and 64 have a disabled person or someone elderly in the household to care for. The role of carer can place great stresses on a woman around the age of retirement, and as this book shows, it is voluntary agencies, not government policies, that offer salvation and a better deal for the carers.

Inevitably, women facing retirement and ageing also face loss. We know that statistically we are likely to outlive our partners, and if we have not yet done so, we must expect to lose our parents. And so, intimations of our own mortality are gathering within us. We are now the front line generation facing old age – not a comfortable thought, but one we have to accept. The important thing is that it should not stop us from building on to our lives, finding new interests, creating new aims. enjoying new freedoms. Now, in retirement, is the time to branch out, whether it is in studying, or travelling or developing a latent talent, or doing voluntary work, perhaps in a field that gives help to other women who are carers or cut off because of language difficulties. Such activities can be of great use to others, and they expand our own horizons. They do not prevent us from growing old, but they help us to do so positively.

There will be times when positive action will not be easy. We may not like our wrinkles or our loss of physical agility. We may not like losing our jobs. We may need time to mourn our losses, big and small. There will perhaps be circumstances when we feel numbed, detached, unable to take any action. We must also allow ourselves this time, to see it as a transition period, not an illness – to lie fallow is also to regenerate. And we know, having seen others grow through bad times, that we can do it as well.

We have to fight the stereotypes in a society that remains obstinately youth and also male dominated. Men grow old too, but are allowed to do so with more power and less restriction than women, who somehow become a source of mockery when they are no longer seen as a source of sexual fantasy. Mother-in-law jokes, seaside cartoon postcards create grotesque battle-axes out of middle-aged women with henpecked, sex-starved husbands as their sidekicks.

Age itself becomes something to be vaguely ashamed of, a situation in which one is barely seen and definately not heard. The American writer Christopher Lasch once pointed out that our generation has 'destroyed the idea that cumulative learning is worthwhile, and that you can discount what a person has learnt simply by living'. It is a comment that applies to men as well as women, and one that must be resisted. By middle age we have learned certain things about ourselves and about society that are enduring and should be heard, things that transcend the dazzle of new technology or even new fashions in thought and behaviour. We may not always be right, but we have a right to be heard.

But to raise our voices as older women, we must have confidence, something that is easily eroded if we take on society's view of us. We can gain that confidence by seeing ourselves in the mainstream of life, not in a backwater. We are not invisible, post-menopausal has-beens, but women with a positive outlook who can shape our own destiny. We can start by looking after our health, by dressing creatively and not apologetically, and enjoying what Margaret Mead once identified as 'post menopausal zest'.

From there, we can develop greater personal strength, perhaps through assertiveness training or some of the other ideas covered in this book. Retirement, with its losses and its gains gives us the opportunity for reassessment. There will be new goals and objectives, new meanings in existing relationships, and new friendships to be made. We can become in better touch with ourselves, less dependent on others for approval.

We can also raise our voices. There are a lot of us to do so. Two-thirds of Britain's pensioners are women. We are voters, and must be recognised as a force to be reckoned with. If we withdrew our care from elderly, infirm and handicapped people, social services would collapse overnight. Yet we are ill-rewarded for our labours: only recently have anomalies in the invalid care allowance been corrected after years of protest and pressure. We are told to be good wives and mothers and to stay at home to preserve family life, yet this too penalises us in later years. Only one-third of retired women receive a full basic State pension in their own right; only 21 per cent of women over 60 receive an employer's pension compared to 60 per cent of men over the age of 65. Such are the penalties for interrupting our work record or giving up outside work completely.

For tax and pension purposes, we are still seen as being dependent on a male partner, even though under 5 per cent of households are made up of working husband and economically inactive wife, and one in eight families are headed by a single parent, the majority being women. These are the issues we have to make a fuss about. And there are many more.

- Our older population increasingly includes people from ethnic minority groups. Barriers of language and culture, and the status of women in these cultures, make ageing especially stressful for some. As in so many areas, it is the voluntary and self-help organisations that are filling the gaps for people from minority groups; but there is a great potential for local authorities to offer resources, and we must urge them to do so in any way we can.

- Medical training must take into account the needs of women from minority groups and indeed doctors must learn to respond more sensitively to the health problems of the elderly generally. We need more time to talk to our doctors, and fewer pills to shut us up. We need well-women clinics for health checks and for information.

- Community care programmes should live up to their name, and not leave the responsibility for caring for elderly relatives and friends 'up to the family', usually meaning a woman. There should be more community and psychiatric nurses, and more back-up from the health service and from local authorities for the carers.

- To enhance the general quality of our lives, we need to see increases, not cutbacks, in public transport, which is relied upon more heavily by women than men of all ages.

- We need more attention to be paid to the run-up to retirement, with all major firms offering pre-retirement courses to male and female employees and their partners. We need more employment agencies for older people who have skills they wish to continue after retirement.

- As summarised in the chapter 'Some money matters', women should campaign for improvements in the social security system to alleviate the problems of poverty in retirement which largely affect women. This is particularly necessary in light of the changes in the system which take effect in April 1988, not to mention the new regulations regarding employers' pension schemes.

The chapter, 'Feeling good, looking good' includes a section on campaigning organisations that are urging change on some of the issues presented in this book and urging women of all ages to take more active part in public life. We can join these organisations, adding our support to their causes. As Maggie Khun, the Convenor of the American group, the Gray Panthers has said. 'The world will change for older women: older women will change the world.' We start off by making changes for ourselves with help from this book.

About the Authors

Helen Franks is a contributor to many women's magazines and newspapers, writing on women's issues, family relationships and health topics. She is author of the book *Prime Time*, on women in the 30-55 age group, and *Goodbye Tarzan*, an investigation into the impact of the women's movement on men.

Caroline Dudley is a journalist who has contributed articles investigating local government issues. She also writes about child care, family relationships, photography and fashion.

Christine Orton is a journalist concerned with social issues and voluntary organisations. She is founder of the National Eczema Society and the author of publications on eczema, caring for elderly people and shared housing in retirement.

Sue Ward is a freelance journalist and researcher. She is the author of books on pensions and social security, writes regularly on these subjects for *The Guardian*, and is associate adviser on pensions to the Industrial Society.

Vivien Donald is a freelance editor and contributor to women's magazines and the author of books about careers.

Acknowledgement

For their help in advising about the manuscript thanks are due to the Information and Policy Department at Age Concern England and, in particular, to Evelyn McEwan for her work on the chapter 'Some money matters'.

About Age Concern

Age Concern England, the publishers of this book as well as a wide range of others, provides training, information and research for use by retired people and those who work with them. It is a registered charity dependant on public support for the continuation of its work.

The three other national Age Concern Organisations – Scotland, Wales and Northern Ireland together with Age Concern England — form a network of over 1,300 independent local UK groups serving the needs of elderly people, assisted by well over 124,000 volunteers. The wide range of services provided includes advice and information, day care, visiting services, voluntary transport schemes, clubs and specialist services for physically and mentally frail elderly people.

Age Concern England
Bernard Sunley House
60 Pitcairn Road
Mitcham
Surrey CR4 3LL
Tel: 01-640 5431

Age Concern Wales
1 Park Grove
Cardiff
South Glamorgan CF1 3BJ
Tel: 02222 371566/371821

Age Concern Scotland
33 Castle Street
Edinburgh EH2 3DN
Tel: 031-225 5000

Age Concern Northern Ireland
128 Great Victoria Street
Belfast BT7 1NR
Tel: 0232 245729

Retiring on your own

Christine Orton considers the challenge of being alone

*M*any women enjoy the independence of being retired when suddenly there is the opportunity to realise dreams and ambitions, from redesigning the garden to writing short stories or taking a degree. All sorts of latent talents which the daily demands of home, work and family may have kept dormant can be rediscovered or developed. There is time to visit friends and favourite places, and to please yourself about what you do and where you go.

But not all of us feel so optimistic about the prospect of aloneness. High on the list of anxieties expressed at pre-retirement and over-50s discussion groups – and sometimes ahead of worries about financial problems and ill health – are fears about the loss of relationships and loneliness. As nearly 50 per cent of women over 65 live alone, compared with only 16 per cent of men, it is a possibility which has to be prepared for.

Dashing to and from a busy job, frantically organising family commitments, domestic routines and social life to fit with working lives, we may often crave for the peace and simplicity of a solitary life. But faced suddenly with being alone through bereavement or divorce, or gradually through the natural lessening of family ties and dependancy, we may find ourselves feeling very differently, remembering with nostalgia the days when we were so busy, needed and surrounded by others.

The loss of important relationships and retirement from a job, with its easy access to daytime companionship and the outside world, can also come at a particularly vulnerable time in life. We are growing older and may feel uncertain about what lies ahead. It may be necessary to create a new identity or to rediscover the person we used to be. This can be a struggle and it may take a while, but as we see all the time among those around us, identity can be achieved, and with tremendous satisfaction and eventual rewards.

Looking at loneliness

Many women these days feel rather guilty about admitting to loneliness. With the modern image in mind of the independent, liberated woman, we tend to think that we *should* be able to cope alone, without the need for someone else's support and company.

Yet, at the same time, we live in a world which in reality is predominantly made up of couples and families. Togetherness, along with youthfulness, are the ideal, and because we are reminded of this in almost every book, newspaper article, film and play, a feeling of loneliness can affect women on their own. Even with lots of friends and interests, it is possible to feel isolated when there is the lack of a particular partnership. Just after a relationship has come to an end, the contrast will be naturally felt all the more strongly. It will take time to grow and put the pieces of a changed life together again in a new and satisfactory pattern.

The person who is feeling stable, confident and optimistic is far less likely to mind being alone than someone who is still reeling from a major bereavement or break-up. We become lonely when we mind being alone, and there is only a thin borderline between the two. Sometimes loneliness may have to be lived with for a while and not fought against.

The temptation is to rush out to lose one's aloneness in all sorts of activities and perhaps a wild search for replacement company. Some may be lucky and fall on their feet quickly, but most of us need time to take stock of our lives and make a calm and realistic appraisal of our needs and potential. It's then that we can start enjoying our aloneness and cope better with any feelings of isolation when they occur, as the following description shows:

《 *Home is the centre of my life, a place to go out to the world from, a place to return to. I enjoy making my flat a pleasant, welcoming and restful place for others as well. Other advantages of living alone are having time and space for myself to read, write, draw, think, learn, do what I feel is right for myself. There are no conflicts about who does the housework, shopping, gardening or pays the bills – I do! I invite friends and family often, and the company is important to me. This includes children. I hope that my new home will be very much a friendly place for others.* 》

In accepting being alone much will obviously depend on the reason behind the situation and our ability to deal with the problems related to being a single person: the death of a partner or parents in retirement; becoming separated or divorced; adjusting to being an 'alien' pensioner.

Remaining single

For women who have never married or lived with anyone else –
preferring instead to remain single – life will change in many
important ways after retirement. In the past, perhaps, it has been
perfectly natural to return after work to an empty flat or house and
relish the orderly atmosphere and the peace and quiet, settling
down alone to TV, music or a book. Friends will probably have
been available when needed; and outings to cinema, theatre,
relatives, pub or restaurant will have broken up evenings and
weekends with pleasant variety. But this comfortable structure is
changed after retirement. When there is no longer the contrast of a
busy working day outside, coming back to an empty home can be
less attractive, as shown in the situation described below.

Kate had worked for many years with her firm, finishing as
head of the sales department. Many of the people in
the office were not close friends, but even so, she enjoyed the day-
to-day contact and sharing of events and experiences.

'Retirement for me meant dropping out of a whole network of
people who had been very much part of my life. Some were part of
my social life as well, even if this was simply lunching together in
the staff canteen or dropping into the pub for a drink on the way
home. After so many years I kept up this contact, especially with
one or two who were real friends. But I did feel out of touch and
missed what was often a superficial but nevertheless very
sustaining daily relationship.'

The loss of status and identity as a career woman and the outside
interest and stimulus of the job also had its affects on Kate.
Eventually she found that apart from keeping up with friends, the
answer was not to hang on to the old life but to start new
involvements of her own, by finding first part-time paid work and
later a voluntary job doing book-keeping and accounting. Her
experience and expertise continued to be put to valuable use, and
she found she enjoyed her increased leisure time all the more.

Loss of parents

As we approach retirement, we are in an age range that may
encompass another kind of loss and sense of loneliness – the death of

parents. Though this is an inevitable event and one we all know we must expect, the reality almost always comes as a shock. If the relationship had been especially close and happy, and if parents have continued to be of prime importance in a daughter's life, then the shock will be all the greater.

Even when there have been tensions and problems, we may have spent many out-of-work hours caring for parents, and there may be deep-rooted feelings of loss. Guilt and regret do not make these any easier to come to terms with. What may have been looked forward to as a release may instead be an unexpected let-down, with retirement from work adding to the feeling of helplessness and lack of purpose.

In the experience of the National Council for Carers and their Elderly Dependants, it is often single women who have spent many years looking after parents who experience the greatest difficulties in being alone.

Often they feel absolutely lost. Even though they may have worked and set up home separately, they have never quite left the role of dependent daughter. Many are resentful, too, because they feel they have missed out by making their parents the centre of their lives, as the NCCED explains:

《 *They may have turned down job promotions to allow more time to be with their parents, or to avoid moving abroad or further from home. They may also have rejected possibilities of other relationships. Now they find themselves alone in later years and often have to rebuild their lives right from scratch.* 》

The NCCED and the other organisations listed on pages 145-7 offer support and counselling for a woman who has spent the whole of her life caring for parents or a relative who has died. Suddenly she has time to think of herself, and this may be something of a shock. The process of adjustment to a new life-style has to be worked through, but gradually there has to be self-discovery and a move to new activities.

Death of a partner

If we are in a happy partnership, whether married or living in a close relationship with a man or woman, retirement years are a time to look forward to and for doing things together. The loss of that partner through death, either shortly before retirement or afterwards, comes as a bitter blow.

One widow whose husband had died shortly after they had both retired felt that it was the practical aspect of life that heightened her feelings of loneliness and loss:

« *We'd been planning to completely redecorate our home from top to bottom, and at first I just couldn't face doing it alone. Also, though we had always shared the chores, there were certain jobs that Frank was better at than me, and vice versa.*

'*We'd also had a double income and shared paying the bills, and I found I was petrified of getting into debt. Bills would arrive and I'd just leave them unopened, frightened of what they'd say.* »

She needed the time and help to come to terms with her grief. But one major turning point came when she started going to carpentry evening classes and found she had real talent for do-it-yourself. She felt much pride when she managed to put up her first set of shelves and use her husband's old electric drill. Fixing door handles, making picture frames and doing all sorts of other odd jobs around the house was part of becoming stronger and learning to cope by herself. Then she was able to move on to paying all those bills that had accumulated.

Divorce and separation

The break-up of a partnership can be as catastrophic as bereavement. No-one likes a relationship to fail, and most of us strive to stay in one, only giving up with great sadness and when the good in whatever we have shared is finally outweighed by the bad.

Divorce or separation that comes late in life is probably hardest of all to come to terms with. There may be a feeling of having wasted life, with less hope of a new beginning. The parting may also coincide with other types of change, such as children leaving home and friends moving away, and of course retirement from work.

There are very particular financial strains for those who are divorced or separated who do not qualify for a special pension like a widow. Even after years of marriage an ex-wife will get no benefit from this if her former husband dies. There is also possible loss of all forms of maintenance once the children have grown up, and no legal entitlement to the family home when they have finished full time education.

Many woman will have chosen to live independently and sell the house anyway. Few want to remain financially dependent on a former partner unless absolutely necessary, and may see no reason why he should not have his share of the proceeds from the house sale.

Caroline had suffered a double loss in that following separation and divorce from her husband, he later died from a sudden heart attack. Now into her 50s, she knows there is the possibility that she will face retirement years alone:

《 *I think one of my main fears has been the children moving away now that they are grown up. They are my only remaining close family and though I won't hang on to them I have worried about feeling lonely.*

'But moving house has made a great difference for me. We have come from the country to a city, and I shall have a chance to get settled in and find new friends before they all take off. If I had left the move till later it would probably have been much more traumatic.

'The move has also helped financially because I made a profit on the house sale, and as this one is smaller the bills are much lower. Now when retirement comes I shall have built a new life for myself and also be able to manage on a lower income. **》**

Growing through mourning

Most people who have experienced the loss of a parent or a partner have suffered bereavement, and must inevitably go through a mourning process. Those who work with bereaved people see mourning divided into four distinct stages.

- The initial reaction is usually shocked disbelief which can last for a long period, while the person may feel very detached from the world or completely at sea.

- Later comes a point of being unable to accept the loss, very often searching for the person who has gone and thinking that he or she is still there.

- Following that, comes a period of despair and depression when the truth finally dawns that the loved one has gone for good. This can be an extremely painful time and there may be a complete loss of interest in living and the feeling that there is no point in going on, no point in doing anything.

- Eventually comes a moment when you find you can remember without necessarily feeling sad, and this is the time to begin life again, to renew old interests and take up new pursuits.

There are all sorts of self-help agencies nowadays to support women in bereavement: Cruse and the National Association for Widows, the National Council for Separated and Divorced, and Gingerbread are just some of the organisations offering support and advice in various ways (addresses on page 145).

The National Marriage Guidance Council (address on page 153) offers help not only to those who are married but also to those who are divorced, separated and bereaved, or simply have problems because they are alone. Other organisations like the Pre-retirement Association (address on page 155) and some branches of Age Concern run discussion groups for older women, where they can talk over worries and experience the fact that they are not alone.

Alone in a foreign culture

The aloneness of later years can be heightened by other factors, some of them geographical. You may have been born in another country, for instance, and still not feel truly at home in the foreign culture and customs you have come to.

Getting older often means a reaching-back to beginnings, and you may yearn to return to the place of your origins, or to be in touch with old friends or relatives far away. But often this is difficult or impossible for financial or other practical reasons. If your ability to speak and understand English is limited, there is also the challenge of adjusting to new ways of living and thinking when you feel you are too old for major changes.

Another problem facing single women about to retire is that retirement may mean loss of home and a completely new way of life – for instance, nurses or community workers whose jobs may have been residential. Counselling Help and Advice Together (address on page 154), an organisation for nurses, says that this difficulty is not as common as it used to be as fewer nursing staff actually 'live in'. But they still do get nurses due for retirement who have nowhere to go apart from a special retirement home for others in the same profession. Very often these women are from another country. On retirement their savings and pension enable them to buy their own flat or cottage; but because they may never have cooked more than a snack for themselves or lived alone, the adjustment to this different way of life can be hard to make.

Pleasing ourselves

The point at which we come to enjoy aloneness is when we start to relish the advantages instead of dwelling on the disadvantages. This isn't something to feel guilty or selfish about, but something to celebrate. After all, despite the joys of companionship, in any close relationship there is usually the debit side, the compromises and sacrifices that are often made to fit in with another person's wishes and way of life.

Now, without constraints, it is possible to develop and explore aspects of ourselves that may never have emerged before. There is also the chance for some self-indulgence – taking breakfast in bed, luxuriating in a long bath, watching what we want on TV rather than what everyone else wants, and so on. Taking positive action and pleasing ourselves helps to capitalise on the advantage of retiring on our own.

The National Marriage Guidance Council book *Alone Again* sees pleasing yourself as an essential part of building up wholeness. Some women find, for instance, they can renew old friendships which didn't fit in with their former lives; interests that may have been put aside many years ago to accommodate someone else can be taken out of mothballs. If a partner never could see the point of going to all those meetings, it may not have stopped you but it certainly took the joy out of attending. Now you can go unhampered by disapproval or feelings of guilt and 'disloyalty' and judge whether the activity really is in your line.

The Open University's (address on page 148) pre-retirement course book lists some of the good as well as the bad feelings you can have about being alone: 'I feel I don't have to put on an act', 'I feel really me', 'I feel relaxed' are some of the items on the list. The handbook also recommends making a diary of feelings when alone, with one column headed: 'Times I was alone and enjoyed it' and the other: 'Times I was alone and didn't enjoy it.' A pattern of high and low spots will emerge, and then some treats – perhaps an outing or a special meal – can be planned for the low times.

Once the outside interest and stimulation of a full-time job has gone, the greatest enemy can be too much unfilled time. It is important to build a new structure for the week with a basic plan to be out so many days or evenings a week, or so many hours a day. There are then contrasts again, and being at home alone becomes more enjoyable.

Weekends are also useful in breaking up stretches of time into more manageable portions. Plan ahead to visit friends or relations – perhaps one weekend out of four – and organise reciprocal visits. There's also the opportunity to plan holidays, perhaps joining with a group of other people.

Deciding where to live

Of course one of the most crucial decisions to make when retiring alone is where to live. You may start to plan a move at this stage in preparation for the changes ahead, but the pros and cons of moving have to be carefully weighed. There are many considerations to take into account.

- Are shops, post office, library, entertainments and doctor's surgery or the hospital in reasonable walking distance or handy for bus or train?
- Are friends and relations who can help in illness or emergency within easy distance?
- Has the area got a friendly and secure atmosphere?
- Are there pleasant parks or good country walks nearby? What about noise? If you have a car, there is also parking to think about.

To move or stay put?

For some people staying put gives a comforting sense of continuity and familiarity, with friends round the corner and a known network of local activities. For others, every room in the home, every scratch in the paintwork or tree in the garden is a painful reminder of the past and there is a real need to move on. Particularly after divorce or separation this may be essential for a sense of independance and starting again. Sometimes the decision is taken out of the woman's hands anyway, as when the family home is sold because children have finished their education and an ex-husband is within his legal rights to ask for his share.

In other situations, the flat or house may simply be too big for your requirements, or much too expensive to run. Do note that there are various local authority schemes to help home-owners maintain their property, though the availability of these grants varies between different areas. A home built before 1919 might merit a grant for repairing foundations or roof, for instance. There are also grants to cover the cost of materials for loft insulation; but do remember that you will need to get approval from the local authority before proceeding with the work. If you think the time may come when you may have to care for an elderly or disabled person in your home, there are also grants available for adapting housing.

This may be the point to take off and realise a long-planned dream – moving to the country if home has always been in town or vice versa. A place familiar from many enjoyable holidays spent there may be the choice or even a move abroad. But remember that this could result in isolation, at least at first. It is not a step to take without a great deal of research and thought, taking into account the considerations outlined above.

If you rent your home from the local authority and want to move within your present locality, the housing department may be able to recommend a housing association in addition to their own accommodation. To move to another area of the country, as a local authority tenant, you will need to have strong social reasons. Apply to the local authority for consideration under the National Mobility Scheme. The authority will have details about this as well as the Tenants Exchange Scheme, which operates between local authorities in different parts of the country.

Moving to a flat or small house in a familiar area may be the answer. But it's important to bear in mind that even if children have left home, they may want to return to stay later on, maybe with partners and grandchildren in tow. At some point there may be a new partnership, a friend to share with or a need to have a lodger for companionship and some extra income. If you do decide to do this and are in receipt of housing benefit, a widow's or supplementary pension, you must find out first whether having a lodger would affect these benefits. Nevertheless, a new home shouldn't be so small as to rule out the possibilities of shared living again one day.

Because you are without a close partner, it isn't essential to live alone, of course. One group of friends clubbed together while they were still relatively young and bought a house in the country for holidays which they could use later for retirement. As one of the group members explained:

« *When we were younger and talked about this as our retirement home, people tended to laugh and think we were being pessimistic thinking so far ahead. But now that retirement is just around the corner we are all really looking forward to spending more time there. Two of our group have been widowed already, and they know they have a familiar place and a familiar setting to settle in.*

'We also have the advantage that we all know each other well and have adjusted to each other's life-styles. Instead of retirement being something to dread, it's a time we are looking forward to. »

Other people may decide to buy or rent a house or flat in a modern purpose-built sheltered or clustered estate. Sheltered housing is available through the housing department of local authorities, some through housing associations and some for purchase from private developers. Sheltered accommodation provides the independance of your own home with the security of an alarm system and sometimes a warden to help when necessary.

Securing your property
It is a sad fact that the older you are, the more vulnerable you can feel in your home, and this is especially true for women on their own. Without ruining life with morbid obsessions about attacks and burglaries, it's sensible to make a home as secure as possible with strong locks on doors and windows and maybe some form of alarm system.

A neighbourly area with at least a few houses nearby will not only give company and a better community feeling but also add to security and safety. Neighbours who can keep an eye on the house, and can be trusted to feed pets or have a key when necessary, can make a lot of difference to settling happily.

Also there is the insurance to consider of your personal possessions and the contents of your home. In fact, most mortgages require that the structure of your home is insured, which of course is a much needed security in the event of burst pipes or flooding. Age Concern England operates a household contents scheme at reasonable rates (address on page 13).

Finding paid work

It isn't necessary, to give up work at 60 or 65 and there are agencies which specialise in finding either paid or voluntary employment for people after they have officially retired. One called Success After Sixty (address on page 149) now considers anyone from the age of 50 because of early retirement or redundancy, or because some women on finding themselves alone at this age need to find another job. As one of the agency interviewers explained:

« *There are many who arrive actually on their 60th birthday, asking us to find them a job because they have no intention of retiring. Others who have been home for a few months come in feeling as if their brains are becoming addled and wanting something to do.*

'*We find jobs for people up to their 70s right across the board, from top executives to cleaners, dinner ladies, gardeners and decorators. There are lots of secretarial and accountancy jobs for women, particularly if they have what we call 'hard skills' such as audio typing, shorthand and word-processing experience.*

'*We have a tea lady on our books at the moment who had to leave the hospital where she was working because of present retirement rules. But we find certain companies actually want the qualities that older people bring – experience, dependability and commitment.* »

The Senior Service Bureau, run by the City of Westminster in conjunction with the local Age Concern places skilled workers, electricians, carpenters, seamstresses in addition to security staff, domestics, babysitters and office clerks. Similar bureaux – although far too few of them – are scattered throughout the country, and their addresses are on page 149. A comprehensive list is also available from the Pre-Retirement Association.

Agencies like this find that some people want a complete change from previous work, others like to continue using the skills they have built up over the years. Some prefer part-time work, so that there is extra income and interest, but time to enjoy leisure, too. Part Time Careers accepts applicants up to age 62 and handles jobs for accountants, book-keepers and secretaries, of whom those with up-to-date experience on electronic typewriters and word processors are easiest to place.

Another route to a part-time job might be by looking at the cards in newsagents' windows, or asking as your local Job Centre or office of Professional and Executive Recruitment, addresses of which will be in your local *Yellow Pages*. For a more challenging opportunity, remember that people with fundraising skills or retired secretaries or accountants are frequently in demand. One occupation which requires people to work a few days now and then is market research, and you will usually see advertisements for this work in local papers.

There is also the possibility of working from home. It may be that in revitalising or developing a talent such as painting, sculpture, macrame, embroidery, carpentry or toy-making you can actually start to earn a living out if it, particularly if what's on offer has an original slant. One woman started making pictures from dried flowers after her husband died and her children left home. A local craft shop took them and after that she had regular orders for them from outlets further afield. There is, of course, considerable scope for someone with cooking, decorating or dress making skills to earn a modest amount of money.

Best selling author Lena Kennedy didn't start writing her books about the old days in the East End of London until she was in her 60s, and painter Beryl Cooke also found fame in later life. It is often the sudden availablity of time that allows women to develop their talents at last – and then find that other people want to pay them for their work!

If you do take a paid job, bear in mind that although you can earn up to a certain amount per week without affecting your state pension your wages will also be subject to income tax. For an up-to-date figure for the Earnings Rule, ask at your DHSS office.

Giving time to the community

The possiblities for voluntary work are endless. Meals on wheels, the Samaritans, Marriage Guidance Counselling and hospital work are among the suggestions that often seem to spring to mind first. Older women with their experience and understanding are certainly needed in these fields. But there is also work with younger children in playgroups, play schemes or parent and toddler clubs. There are also local art centres, wanting help with running workshops of all sorts – for instance, pottery, drama, or photography. Voluntary organisations need counsellors, accountants, book-keepers, computer buffs.

Many community organisations are self-help, set up by members themselves and kept going by their own efforts. Being asked to go on a committee may be something we tend to shy away from at first. But in the end we get back as much as we give, and find that though such activities are often hard work and demanding, the fact that we are needed and active is rewarding and stimulating.

Caroline who had moved to a new area was asked by a neighbour to join a committee planning the local summer carnival. She went along because she didn't like to say no, but also she thought she might meet more people and get involved with the community: 'I really enjoyed it, we had a sponsored walk along the canal towpath and pub socials to raise money for the event, plus lots of committee meetings. It was fun and made me feel useful and wanted. It also meant that I became much more familiar with the area I lived in and the people around.'

It's possible to go on volunteer holidays. You pay a small fee for board and lodging, and then find yourself doing things as varied as archeological digs in the West Country or maintaining the duckeries at Leeds Castle. The British Trust for Conservation Volunteers say they welcome anyone from 17 to 70 (address on page 152). There is a similar organisation that runs projects in Scotland; and the National Trust also uses volunteers in many aspects of its work.

There are possiblities for a great range of skills to be used in volunteering and for a lot of enjoyment to be had into the bargain. A local volunteer centre or Age Concern group should be able to match up talents with projects that need them.

Developing new interests

Every woman who has found herself alone and lonely knows that sinking feeling when told: 'You ought to join something, find a new interest, go to evening classes'. The thought of a cold classroom on an autumn evening is the last thing she probably wants!

Yet making the effort can have surprising practical as well as social and intellectual benefits. These days women try all sorts of classes, from plumbing and electrical repairs to car maintenance. Useful, too, would be classes in book-keeping and accountancy which would help in sorting out the often difficult financial problems of managing on your own. For some women at this stage, cooking can become an absorbing hobby rather than the necessity of life it was when there were others to feed – a social pleasure or simply a personal indulgence.

The Greater London Association for Pre-Retirement (address on page 154) publishes *Something Different To Do* which lists unusual interests and organisations to contact all over the country. For instance, there is a garden history society which campaigns for conservation of historic gardens and arranges visits and conferences, or an association for inland waterways needing volunteers to preserve Britain's canal heritage.

There are great opportunities for older women now, too, and after retirement, there is more time to take advantage of them. The University of the Third Age, the Workers Educational Association and the Open University offer a wide range of courses (addressses on page 148). Many universities also run holiday courses with accommodation provided. A degree in your fifties, sixties and seventies may not lead to a new career, but it will certainly result in a growing confidence and greater fulfilment.

Getting together with others

Though taking up an interest for its own sake may also lead to new friends and a good social life, it can be helpful or necessary to join a club purely for emotional support or to forge fresh contacts.

Luckily there are associations for just about every type of person, problem and interest nowadays. Some, like Cruse, tend to be more for counselling and advice. Others, like the National Council for the Divorced and Separated, are more social, with meetings, discos and so on (address on page 147).

It can be very supportive to meet others in the same situation as yourself. For a start it makes you feel much less alone, but also through talking and listening to others you learn how they cope, emotionally as well as practically, and this can put problems into perspective.

There are, of course, lots of over-60s and pensioner groups. But not everyone wants to mix purely with their peers at this age any more than at any other. Groups bonded through interests or situations rather than the fact that members happen to be over 60 may be far more suitable.

A good example are the reminiscence and life history projects now active in many areas of the country. These often involve school children, teenagers, middle-aged and retired people working together to research the history of an area and collect old photos and mementoes. Reminiscence is often an important aspect of the clubs run for people from various ethnic minority groups. Older people from the Caribbean, China, Asia, and India meet together and have a chance to discuss their culture and their memories.

For a growing number of older women, a great support in building up a sense of independence and self-esteem has been the a growth of the feminist movement, and there is more on this in the chapter 'Feeling good, looking good'.

Making new relationships

Even if there is no close partnership in our lives during youth or middle age, there is no reason to suppose this will always be the case; nor is there any need to be ashamed of wanting a close and interdependent relationship. However well we learn to cope alone, most people need and miss the warmth, loving care and release of emotion that a close partnership, particularly a sexual one, can bring into our lives.

The right person may just happen to come along, or it may be necessary to take certain steps to help this happen. Whereas people once felt that there must be a certain desperation in answering magazine 'lonely heart' advertisements or in going along to a dating bureau, nowadays these channels are seen as a practical way of finding a new friend or suitable lover. As the director of an introduction agency for people over forty in North London explains:

《 *Finding a partner can become more difficult the older people get, and retirement from work means one place less where there is the possibility of meeting someone new. Some women who have always had a career only get to think about the need for closer relationships after that finishes. Others are widowed or divorced, and hate being the odd one out among friends who are all couples.*

'Our agency isn't just for marriage, though. We introduce people for friendship and we put women in touch with other women. But we do suggest that people don't rush into new relationships after a major emotional crisis such as bereavement or divorce. Sometimes it is necessary to wait as long as two years before the upheaval and upset dies down to a level where you are really ready to cope again. 》

One woman in her late 50s, who went all round Europe on her own after the break-up of her marriage as a sort of test for strength, took the philosophy that it was better to live life as if you didn't expect to meet anyone special. Then if anything did happen, it would simply be an added bonus.

Certainly the worst way to come to terms happily with being alone is to struggle constantly against it, always waiting for someone else to come along and take away our loneliness. The irony is that once we no longer desperately need another person but really enjoy life for its own sake we are far more likely to make a satisfying relationship. Having learnt to cope happily on our own, the likelihood is that we find we are not alone after all.

Further reading

Something Different To Do
> Greater London Association for Pre-Retirement, address on page 154

Alone Again
> Angela Williams, National Marriage Guidance Council, 1977, address on page 153

Depression, The Way Out of Your Prison
> Dorothy Rowe, Routledge & Kegan Paul, 1983

On Your Own
> Jean Shapiro, Pandora, 1985

Survival Guide for Widows
> June Hemer and Ann Stanyer, Age Concern England, 1986

Housing Options for Elderly People
> David Bookbinder, Age Concern England, 1987

Sharing Your Home
> Christine Orton, Age Concern England, available September 1987

Buyer's Guide to Sheltered Housing
> National Housing and Town Planning Council and Age Concern England, 1985

Recall Slides and Tapes
> Help the Aged, address on page 155

Part-time work and Social Security Benefits NI 242 DHSS

National Mobility Scheme
> Department of the Environment

Accommodation for Elderly People – Housing Schemes Factsheet
Improving and Repairing Your Home Factsheet
Sheltered Housing for Sale Factsheet
> Age Concern England, free with A4 SAE.

Retiring together

Caroline Dudley discusses the challenge of sharing retirement

*W*hen a couple are ready to retire together, the outlook may be a rosy one: lots of time to share, new interests to follow, old ones to be resumed. But retiring is more often a one-sided affair, with a wife still perhaps in part-time employment or used to her own routine during her husband's working hours. While it may not necessarily be true that absence makes the heart grow fonder, there's no doubt that too much unaccustomed togetherness can put a marriage under strain. This goes for couples of the same sex too, and for friends who live together.

Even the happiest of couples need some space between them. Some partnerships have endured only because of the absence of one, most usually the husband, on business trips or, at least, his lack of presence in the house during the day. Couples in this kind of situation, suddenly confronted by each other's moods, prejudices, foibles, and, indeed, continued presence day after day, may find themselves facing a great new emotional challenge at a time in life when they thought they knew everything they needed to know about their relationship.

It is a challenge most particularly of our times and particularly relevant to marriage. At the beginning of the century in the United Kingdom, two out of three men aged 65 were still at work, whereas by 1984 this figure had decreased to less than one in ten, which means that retirement, for those with the youth and vigour to enjoy it, is a recent phenomenon. As a result of the dramatic fall in infant and childhood mortality rates since 1900, there are now 11 million people in this country aged over 60. This, allied to the economic climate which has either led or forced many employees to retire early, means that more people than ever before can look forward to many years of active and purposeful life ahead, following their disengagement from full-time work.

This is why pre-retirement planning is sometimes known as 'mid-life planning' – an appropriate term in view of the fact that present-day retirement can span almost as many years as a working career. Planning, or at least mental preparation, is needed for this transition, whether we intend to have an active retirement, or just 'sit and do nothing'. About 10,500 men each year die less than two years after their retirement. Many will have taken the 'ostrich' attitude, refusing to discuss or even acknowledge its approach. A survey carried out by the British Market Research Bureau revealed that nearly half of Britain's working population refuse to think about their retirement, with one in three couples admitting that they never even discuss old age between themselves. Retirement, when it comes, hits these people unnecessarily hard, and can propel them into a downward spiral of lethargy and depression, leading to premature death.

People 'at risk' from retirement

Studies have shown that the men most vulnerable to problems in adjusting to retirement are career 'high-fliers' and the self-employed. These men, either forgetting or not realising that work is but a component of life and not a reason for it, are likely to have spent too much time working, to the exclusion of family and leisure activities. The third high-risk group comprises manual workers without hobbies and interests, whose entire social contact has been based on their workplace. These men, suddenly faced with being at home all the time, feel threatened by the fact that life seems to be shutting all the doors on them.

Almost everyone, man or woman, feels some sense of misgiving at the prospect of retirement, and for men in particular, it can seem like being 'thrown on the scrap heap'. It is indeed, to some extent, a loss situation, and given society's reverence, however misplaced, for earning power as a barometer of social status, it is hardly surprising that the change in role from breadwinner to pensioner comes as a bitter blow in many cases. Women are generally less tied to their work and more able to adjust to retirement (though as more and more women devote great energy and interest to a career, this is changing). They may know, intellectually, that their partner is less adaptable, but may not find the reality easy to deal with.

Audrey Baker, tutor for the National Marriage Guidance Council (address on page 153), says that although long-established marriages do not necessarily founder at retirement, many couples make themselves miserable by not communicating. It helps if couples can think in advance about what retirement will be like: to think individually about what they'd like to happen, and even more importantly, to talk to each other about what they'd like to happen. It makes so much difference if you tell each other what you hope for, rather than expecting your partner to know, or to assume that your partner wants and expects the same things.

« *After all, a couple's lives may have been built on a lot of separateness. The individuals may function well in different compartments, and while they may have inhabited the same house for 30 years, believing they are together, they may, in fact, not be together as far as their hopes and expectations go, so it is terribly important that they voice these things to their partners. There are a lot of positive aspects to retirement, but there is a negative side too, and if this is not discussed and given a proper airing, it can go bad, and ruin the rest of life. If a husband and wife can only tell each other how uncomfortable they feel about the change, and how odd it makes them feel, not endlessly or every day, but just to give a place to the fact, then they have a good chance of staying on a fairly positive course.* »

Planning for retirement

Many people spend more time planning a holiday than in preparing for retirement, which may well occupy up to thirty years of life. Pre-retirement planning can minimise the shock and subsequent demoralisation which can accompany retirement, and can help those about to retire to develop a constructive philosophy.

The first pre-retirement courses were held in the United States in 1949, but it is only in the last ten to fifteen years that the need for them has been recognised in the United Kingdom. It has been established that no more than ten per cent of retirees in the UK receive any kind of retirement counselling. Some large companies and local authorities provide pre-retirement courses, either by inviting specialist lecturers in, or by sending the employees on courses which usually last for one or two days. Ideally, spouses should be invited to participate too, but unfortunately, this does not always happen. A very few forward-looking companies follow up on these courses by allowing employees to cut down to a four-day week from six months before retirement, reducing again to a three-day week in the last three months. This smoothes the transition very well for the employee who is retiring, but the practice is still far from widespread.

One of the most important topics is how to plan your finances for a comfortable retirement. As this is often linked up with annuities, endowment policies and private pension plans, several of the major life assurance companies, such as the Legal and General Assurance Society (address on page 155) run their own courses as a service for their prospective pensioners, for groups of employees of large companies, or for individuals from smaller companies. They invite outside speakers to cover financial topics so that course participants can obtain unbiased investment advice. As their retirement counselling manager explained, Legal and General has over one million people either paying towards or drawing out pensions, so it makes sense for them to offer pre-retirement courses which are paid for either by the individuals themselves or their employers.

Local education authorities also run courses which typically require attendance for two hours a week for six weeks, in the evenings. Sessions cover such topics as living on a pension, investments, income tax; staying healthy and active in retirement; assessment of local community services; employment prospects for paid or voluntary work; accommodation and the pros and cons of moving house after retirement. The advantage of the local authority course is that the information relates to what is available in your locality, and people are welcome to attend as couples or singly.

The Pre-Retirement Association (address on page 155) runs day or weekend courses for the employees of large companies; and as the PRA has a countrywide network of speakers, these can be set up anywhere in the UK in response to demand. There are also retirement holiday weeks organised by the PRA at Pontin's, South Devon Holiday Centre, costing around £100 per person per week. These courses attract both couples and single people, and a holiday atmosphere prevails, as the lectures are less intensive than they must be in the shorter courses. They take place in the mornings, while the afternoons are given over to discussion groups which follow on from the morning's lecture. There are also sessions on developing hobbies such as gardening, bridge, golf and ballroom dancing, and talks on skin care and make-up given by experts. As with most pre-retirement education, individual financial counselling is a strong feature of the retirement holiday weeks.

If you would prefer to plan your retirement from the comfort of your home, the Open University's study pack *Planning Retirement* covers more than sixty topics including ways to examine your attitudes about time and being retired (address on page 148).

Sharing the housework

One of the basic things to be negotiated is the matter of running the home, now that there are two adults spending so much time in it. Couples who have a history of sharing the domestic duties and 'mucking in' together, find that the transition happens smoothly. Many retired couples say that they have always shared the chores, but even a couple of the same sex sharing a home may have allocated each other certain jobs over the years, and need now to rethink who does what.

The newly retired partner is often prepared to do more around the house, but may not realise that there is a difference between being helpful and fully sharing domestic responsibilities. Many men basically have a Walter Mitty attitude to housework. Where the roles have been strictly divided, a man may feel like a stranger in his own house, lacking the domestic experience to share the chores. To compensate, and, anxious to preserve his patriarchal status, he may become querulous and demanding instead. This is most likely to happen where the wife has not worked outside the home. We have been brought up to regard the house as our domain, and, despite wanting a man to pull his weight, can resent the feeling of being usurped. It's one thing to have an assistant, another to feel one is being taken over.

As with any situation, facing up to the facts, confronting and questioning your fears can help. What are you afraid of? Why does it matter if your husband gets the lunch and drops the crumbs on the floor, so long as he clears up afterwards? These are questions we can ask ourselves, noting our own resistance to change and our need to control a situation. It is possible to make a break-through and find what at first appeared to be a problem turns into a sensible and satisfactory arrangement.

In fact, studies on groups of retired people have shown that as the years progress, the demarcation lines between the accepted division of roles begins to blur, and there is more sharing of domestic tasks. It makes sense to share chores, because in doing so we are learning how to cope on our own, should we outlive a partner. A man who has skills of basic cooking, cleaning and mending already within his grasp is better prepared; and by the same token, retirement provides an opportunity for women to learn some 'male' skills, such as wiring plugs, changing tap washers, and other household repairs so that, if she should be widowed, she will not feel totally helpless.

What to do after breakfast?

Outlining a routine can help a lot to give each day some shape. It doesn't have to be followed slavishly, which can happen when a man wants to impose a schedule and organise it as formally as he has organised his work. All that time and space without any shape' is frightening, and life on a permanent weekend is no fun. Even an agreement about the time you might get up in the morning, and who gets up first, for instance, is important. Perhaps plan a special activity for the morning – if you are very energetic, and enjoy swimming, you might find a local bath which offers early morning swimming. This is often free to pensioners.

If you have always shared a daily newspaper, now's the time to have one each, to read and discuss over breakfast. There are radio programmes to listen to on a regular basis, to take away the aimlessness of a lie-in every morning. Beyond this start to the day, there are many activities to plan.

Many women are filled with trepidation at the thought of their husbands' retirement because they just want to do nothing. What are they going to do after breakfast and where are they going to do this nothing? Most women say they can cope with the idea of afternoons and evenings, holidays and all the rest; but the thought of 9 am on a weekday when a couple look at each other and the husband says he's got nothing to do fills many wives with horror.

Even though men, traditionally, have more time for hobbies than women, especially when children are small, by retirement age many women who are not working full-time have made a programme of daytime social and leisure activities for themselves. This is part of the life that we have created, and which gives us pleasure, support and autonomy. There is no reason why we should not continue our activities, if we choose to do so, after our partners have retired. Ideally, this is a subject to be discussed during the pre-retirement stage. But it doesn't always work out easily, as shown in the situation outlined below.

Elizabeth and Harry had been married for ten years, both for a second time. Harry had recently retired as a director of a multi-national company, and, apart from spending more time gardening, had not developed any replacement interests. Elizabeth works two days a week in a friend's boutique which she enjoys, as it gives her a little pin money and some independent social contact. Harry cannot accept the fact that she has activities and commitments that do not directly relate to him, and keeps up a constant pressure on her to give up her job so that they can spend all their time together. This alienates Elizabeth even more, so that she now regards her job as an oasis in a desert of coping with Harry's lack of direction.

It is easy to see why Elizabeth feels this way, and needs a lot of tact and patience to cope with what she perceives as her husband's unreasonable childishness. To be the captain of industry one day, and following your wife around the supermarket the next represents a major change in role, and can cause a man to feel confused about his self-image.

A marriage guidance tutor also explains Elizabeth and Harry's situation as being a direct result of the demands placed upon middle and senior management in today's society where men are expected to give their 'all' to their jobs and 'breathe the company'. This means that a man sacrifices every other aspect of himself to the job and forgets his other roles, such as father, son, brother, friend and lover, and also forgets that in his teens, perhaps, he liked playing the piano, going to football matches, singing in the choir and writing short stories. This leaves him with a personality that is highly developed in one direction at the expense of the rest.

As shown with Elizabeth and Harry, the man feels very much threatened, as he's lost his job, by retiring, and it now looks as though he is losing his wife as well. In fact, even without knowing it, he may be looking to her as a vehicle by which he might rediscover his lost self, which didn't have the chance to blossom earlier. As his wife has a broad range of interests, he instinctively knows she has things to teach him, so he needs her even more at this time in his life than ever before. In order to help him, she will have to devote some of her time to defining something that he would really like to do, and doing it with him.

If Harry wanted to play bridge, they could learn together, join a club, and he might find a chance to play bridge in the daytime when she was unavailable, and eventually get to mind less about her other activities. From these bits of activity, a richer life could develop; but it is vital that whatever Harry and Elizabeth choose is something they both really want to do and not a situation where she goes along with it in a patronising way, and then leaves him high and dry. Another option would be for her to negotiate some 'good quality' time for them to spend together, when they give each other the best of their attention. This is not always easy, especially when the relationship is going through a sticky patch, but if they can feel close from time to time, the pulling-back will happen less, and Elizabeth could reassure Harry that just because she wants to do things for herself doesn't mean that she doesn't want him.

In Harry's case, a pre-retirement course could have been of great value in encouraging him to accept his impending retirement and helping him decide how to redirect his energies before he finished working. He could then have discussed the matter more openly, and received some of the reassurance and guidance he needed. As it is, Elizabeth could perhaps encourage him to do some voluntary work or find part-time employment to redefine his identity and meet new people.

Adjusting to being together

When both partners retire at more or less the same time, the adjustment is often easiest to organise. Decisions about balancing the time between independent interests and activities can be undertaken jointly.

Marjorie aged 66, arranged to retire from her job a week before Tom. They enjoy being at home together: she attends keep-fit classes and meets her former colleagues for coffee once a fortnight, while Tom spends more time on gardening and playing whist. Because he also enjoys snooker, four years ago Marjorie took up the game, so that they could play together. Tom then decided to join a club which admits women (not all of them do) and snooker has become a shared interest. They also belong to an enjoying retirement group run by Network, a local community organisation, which arranges outings, debates, and lectures in response to members' ideas. Although money is not plentiful, Marjorie and Tom are finding retirement great fun.

Retiring around the same time as your partner isn't always the best answer. Women who enjoy housework but have had a full-time job say that they look forward to having time to do things like get the carpet shampooed or make new curtains without someone else being in the way.

Elaine a retired civil servant who had worked all her life, felt she made a mistake in retiring at the same time as her friend Louise who had always opted out of the cooking and cleaning in favour of gardening and doing the decorating. After a job which had taken up all of her energies, Elaine didn't realise how long she would need to do all the jobs she had been putting off for years. She hadn't even begun to sort things out when Louise retired a month later.

Furthermore, she wasn't too keen on having to shop and prepare three meals a day when she'd been so organised before, and had done the minimum of cooking. After a few months of getting the house in order, Elaine became as restless as the stereotyped male executive and persuaded Louise to move out into the country. As she later explained:

'It didn't work. We found it oppressive, inconvenient and village life is horribly nosey. I realise now that we were trying to find an interest for ourselves and had done the classic thing of looking for it in a new environment which actually involved more adjustment and less ease than if we had stayed where we were. I think if I had had more time to myself when I first retired I wouldn't have made that mistake and would have looked for interests nearer home.'

Developing separate interests is certainly a way to keep the balance in a partnership, as shown in the situation of Donald and Pat, outlined below. Although married for more than forty years, both partners are very independent. They enjoy being together, but not for every minute of the day.

Donald retired first at the age of 56, after attaining the maximum pensionable service with an insurance company, but then took another job, with less responsibility, as book-keeper for a local garage. After his second retirement eight years later, he was again 'let down lightly', by doing a few days' work a month on market research. He had been fully retired for three years and happily occupied with reading and local committee work before Pat retired as home help supervisor for a London borough.

Pat's job had already brought her into contact with the problems people face when they retire and feel that just because they've stopped working, they've dropped out of society. She also realised that she had an advantage over her mother's generation because she had worked, and was more inclined to go out and do things in her retirement.

'The thing most people fear when they retire, is being dragooned into playing bingo and having sing-songs, but there's no need for life to be like that. There are lots of hobbies you can take up and many of them cost very little.'

If you have been very much home-based, you may need some encouragement from your partner in getting involved in community activities or a hobby; and it may be necessary, in order to avoid being over dependent on another person. It could be that your husband has announced his intention to spend his retirement playing golf or on some other activity which, for one reason or another, excludes you, and you would welcome more time spent together. If so, say how you see retirement as affecting you, and try to discuss how you can organise more time together, balanced with time spent on independent interests. Perhaps you're the one who needs to broaden your horizons. There are many ideas about how you can do this, discussed throughout the book.

It is important to say how you feel and let your husband know of your need for overt support and encouragement. As well as the opportunity for his own outside activities, your husband may also need an 'escape hatch' – a study, a greenhouse or workshop, or at least time alone, so that he, too, can potter about and recharge the batteries.

If your husband retires on a Friday, it is unrealistic to think that your great new life together will take off with a flourish the following Monday; but the good news is that if you can think in terms of allowing yourselves time to renegotiate the way you live together, the chances are that you will both have adjusted to the new situation within about two years.

Molly and George are an example of a couple who needed to work at the adjustment. Molly retired seven years before her husband George, when she was 54, on the grounds of ill-health. She had much enjoyed her work as classroom assistant in a school for handicapped children, but after an operation and slow recovery to full health, she was persuaded by her family not to return to work.

At first, she felt bereft, because all her friends were working and the people she met during the day were a generation older. She was very depressed, until they moved house, which gave her something to concentrate on, so she could settle down to the fact that she had retired. Previously, she had felt that the activities provided for retired people were not sufficiently mind-stretching and seemed to be based on younger people's vision of what pensioners wanted. But recently a lot more interesting projects, such as the University of the Third Age (address on page 148) had got off the ground, and she was enjoying two of the courses being run locally.

George took early retirement at the age of 59, and there's no doubt that he felt he had been pushed – he had loved his job as a laboratory manager for a large company, but the firm was making massive redundancies, and he had to go. They gave him a bit of consultancy work for the first year, but after that he didn't know what he would do.

George's retirement led Molly to rethink her situation. She had never regarded herself as a very organised person, and didn't even consider she had a routine; but when George retired, realised that she did have a kind of pattern. 'I like having him at home, but I also need a day to myself now and again, just to be able to think my own thoughts.' Her observation pinpoints what many wives feel: that life changes radically once their husbands retire. It may be very nice to have them at home, but the pattern of life does change.

George feels that he has to make a decision on how to approach the next phase: 'Though I didn't wish to retire, the first three months were like a holiday. But then I began to find it rather unsatisfying, so I'm now looking for a job, either part-time or full time, but if that doesn't work out, I shall get involved in voluntary work.'

Although he is taking a positive attitude, it is clear that George's self-image has been shaken. He is still talking in terms of a new career, rather than retiring, and this is not surprising in view of the work ethic, which tells us that the only 'proper' way for a man to spend his time is in productive employment and makes it very difficult for men to take up interests purely for the enjoyment.

One thing George has discovered is that there is no shortage of things for retired people to do. Apart from special interest groups, like the Royal Horticultural Society and the National Trust, there are courses run by the local authority, with reduced rates for senior citizens, and there are many voluntary organisations that need help. The problem seems to be choosing the most appropriate activity or organisation, as both George and Molly feel they have a lot to offer the community.

Improving your relationship

If you and your partner have problems which make you deeply unhappy, don't gloss over them in the hope that they will go away. It is easy for resentment and bitterness to develop, and then a withdrawal from the relationship, when retirement could be a very exciting and enjoyable time of life. Marriage guidance counselling has helped thousands of couples to renew their relationships, though there may be a waiting list and a delay of several weeks or months before counselling is offered. The value of counselling is that it allows you to state your points of view to each other, before a trained and unbiased third party who can help you to resolve the issues that bother you.

Another approach is to enrol for a Marriage Enrichment Course. These are weekend courses designed for couples who feel they have a stable relationship, and want to work at improving it, particularly through communication skills. Although run under the auspices of the Anglican church, the courses welcome couples of all religions and none. Each course, which costs about £80 per couple, is run by a leader couple, accredited by the Association of Marriage Enrichment (address on page 153).

Enjoying sex

Today, there is an attitude which says that if you don't want an active sex life, there must be something wrong with you. In fact, research in America has shown that many very happy and successful marriages, whether of five or thirty-five years' duration, include very little sex. If this comes as no surprise to you, then you can skip this section. If you want to change your sex life, if perhaps your needs are different to your partner's, then read on.

Previous generations were brought up in an age when it was thought not 'respectable' – especially for women – to enjoy sex; and men and women over 50 or so were expected to be together 'for companionship', to the exclusion of any sexual activity. Fortunately, these repressive attitudes are vanishing fast, and there's no reason why sexual relationships should not flourish after retirement. Recent press coverage was given to a newly married couple, both aged 85, who arrived at their hotel to discover that they had been allocated twin beds. They complained and asked why they were being treated differently from other couples.

Of course enjoying lovemaking also applies to lesbians. Perhaps in later life a long-standing partnership with another woman can be expanded to include sex now that there is more time and more confidence. Some women who form a relationship with another woman in middle age say that they discover a new kind of fulfilment and a sense of equality with another person that they felt escaped them before.

Enjoyment of heterosexual activity does not need to diminsh with age; and, in fact, many women gain greater satisfaction from sex in their later years than formerly, when they were subject to the pressures and distractions of raising a family, or fear of an unwanted pregnancy. Men, too, can experience an increase in libido once the pressures of work have ceased. Some changes, however, both physical and psychological, are to be expected, but given general good health, there is no reason why we should not enjoy making love well into old age.

The confidence that often comes with maturity can help us to voice our sexual preferences to our partners in a way which we may have been inhibited about in the past, and the ability to communicate sexual needs gives a good foundation for a satisfying relationship.

Adjusting to physical changes

After the menopause there is a progressive thinning of the vaginal walls and a drying out of the mucous membrane which provides lubrication to the vagina. This lack of lubrication may result in a burning sensation after intercourse, and apart from making sure your partner takes care to arouse you sufficiently, the application of K-Y jelly or Sensuelle, obtainable from chemists, may bring relief. There are other aids to dryness discussed in the chapter 'Taking care of yourself'.

Though men do not experience a menopause, natural ageing takes its toll. Physically, men tend to find that they take longer to get an erection, and ejaculation results in less semen than when they were younger. Some men feel easily humiliated when they discover they are impotent in middle age. There may be special reasons for it. Medication taken to relieve high blood pressure can cause impotence, for example, and a visit to the doctor may be worthwhile to check on this – sometimes a change to another brand may be suggested. But be aware that doctors themselves can feel threatened when they are consulted about sexual problems and may not be very helpful.

Premature ejaculation, another common problem, is often caused by anxiety as to whether the erection will be maintained. It can result from not having sex often enough, and can be treated with a system of exercises. During intercourse, the man withdraws his penis from the vagina when he feels he's about to ejaculate. Then he or his partner squeezes the tip of the penis. By doing this he will become able to maintain control for gradually increasing amounts of time.

Another technique for delaying ejaculation is for the man to practice tensing his muscles to stop the flow while urinating. This tensing should be held for a count of five, then released, and repeated several times. Having got the feel of the exercise, it can be repeated anywhere, and should be done many times a day. Apart from the aim of delaying ejaculation, it gives increasing bladder control, which can help to eliminate 'waterworks' trouble later in life. For more details of how to cope with these and other sexual problems, see the booklist at the end of the chapter.

Exploring alternatives

Having achieved orgasm, many men find later in life that the interval before the next erection increases to hours, or even days; but this is no reason for abandoning sexual activity. (Women do not lose the ability to achieve orgasms, and some may still lubricate naturally after the menopause.) Many men become anxious about the lack of spontaneous erection and diminished ejaculation, and fear they are becoming impotent. Burdened by the fear that some 'performance', of which they feel incapable, is expected, and therefore that their 'manliness' is threatened, they may get so miserable and anxious that they realise their worst fears, by becoming unable to have an erection and then hiding behind the idea that 'I'm an old man now, so what can I expect?' For a woman who still wants an active sex life, this is hardly satisfactory.

Many couples continue to enjoy sexual intercourse once or twice a week into old age, but some people have neither the inclination or ability for this, and of course in a long relationship we do adjust to our partner's needs. But if you want to improve the quality of your sex life, you have nothing to lose and everything to gain. It's a question of a new approach.

For a start, making love does not have to consist of vaginal penetration; and time spent reassuring, cuddling, caressing, fantasising and laughing together can be enjoyed for its own sake, or to reduce the tension so that you can relax sufficiently to enjoy intercourse. By exploring your own body and finding out, by masturbation, what feels good to you, you can guide your partner, so that he is able to arouse you to a climax, even if he does not have an erection.

Often an erection is more easily maintained in the morning, and since there may well be no reason to get up early, both of you can enjoy the luxury of making love then. The name of the game is fun, and mutual affection, so don't have anything to do with recriminations, or things being anybody's 'fault'. If you have difficulty in achieving orgasm, try not to feel guilty, and don't blame yourself either. Remember, it is something you want to resolve with your partner if possible. It is a sad fact that unspoken resentment is the commonest cause of sexual problems in middle-aged couples.

One way to regain verbal and physical communication is to

show warmth by touching more often, sitting close together when watching television, and taking the trouble to look nice, not just when you are going out, but to please each other when you are at home together.

The National Marriage Guidance Council offers sexual therapy and also publishes a booklet about this type of counselling. The Association of Sexual and Marital Therapists specialises in helping couples come to terms with both the psychological and physical aspects of their relationships (addresses on page 153). You might also find it helpful to attend a women's sexuality workshop, run by the Redwood Association (address on page 144). The course content includes: exploring fantasy, sexual response, body image, and a look at some of the underlying feelings which prevent us from reaching our sexual potential.

Enjoying your leisure

One of the great luxuries of retirement is the increased leisure time it brings. Some people do not feel ready for this, and need to find voluntary or part-time paid work to give themselves a feeling of worth and to supplement an inadequate pension. For many people, however, one of the bonuses of retirement is the ability to get off the treadmill and stop rushing. Some find that they do slow down somewhat, and this is no bad thing – after all, what is the point of continuing to play a game of 'Beat the Clock' from morning till night?

The active contemplation of a flower, a butterfly, children in the park, or the birds on the bird table are all part of the joy of living, to be appreciated now as never before. Indulging in passive leisure activities such as reading and listening to the radio cost nothing and can seem a luxury after a lifetime of sticking to a working schedule.

Adult education classes can increase skills in subjects like photograph, badminton, or a language, often leading to joining a club or group devoted to that interest. For more details of educational opportunities in retirement see the chapter 'Feeling good, looking good'.

There are of course things to see, places to visit. If you are within reach of London and enjoy the theatre, there is a scheme run by the

West End Theatre Group – membership is £1 a year, and entitles you to matinee tickets at half price. If you live outside London, ask if your local theatre operates a similar scheme, and if not perhaps you can persuade the management to start one.

Visiting museums, the zoo, stately homes and historic sites, can now be enjoyed during the week when they are less crowded. Most of these offer reduced price admission to pensioners, and you can obtain details of concessions from your local Citizen's Advice Bureau or town hall welfare department. In some areas of the country, taking day trips into town or country on public transport is cheaper thanks to free or reduced price travel for pensioners. Your local bus or rail station can supply booklets on places to visit, or country walks within reach of big cities.

Sport is no longer the exclusive province of young people, and the Sports Council runs a campaign called '50 Plus', to encourage older people either to continue to participate in sport, or to start now. Particularly popular are swimming, cycling and walking. Some swimming baths offer an over-50s afternoon, once a week, with a swim, plus tea and biscuits for a minimal charge like 20p. Maybe your local baths have a similar scheme. The Sports Council also provides speakers for pre-retirement courses in addition to its funding of local initiatives, so if you'd like to start a sports project in your area, ask them for help (address on page 156).

Leisure centres in Greater Manchester have a schedule of concessions, which are available to senior citizens at certain times and days of the week. Most offer more than 50 per cent off the cost, not only of the activity, such as badminton, karate, table tennis, swimming or rowing, for example, but also of the equipment: badminton racquets, table tennis bats and rowing boats. When claiming a concession, you will be asked to produce your pension book as proof of entitlement.

Birmingham has a scheme called Passport to Leisure, which is also in operation or being planned in other areas, including Norwich and Gloucester. This offers concessional rates for leisure centres and adult educational courses to retired people and those receiving supplementary and unemployment benefit. For schemes in your area, enquire at the town hall or the library.

Help with transport

All these outside activities are fine, as long as you can get to them. Ask at your local post office or council for information on obtaining a bus pass; and for a leaflet on how to get a Senior Citizen's Railcard, ask at your local railway station, or British Rail registered travel agent. To qualify for travel concessions you have to be 60 and will have to give proof by showing your pension book or a special card. A Railcard may also entitle you to reduced fares on Sealink ships to the Channel Islands and Ireland and for travelling by rail and sea to 17 Continental countries.

With these concessions the cost of transport is less of a problem than availability. In the suburbs and, especially in rural areas, the frequency of public transport can make all the difference between attending an activity that you enjoy and spending cold, wet afternoons waiting at the bus stops. If there is a need for improved services in your area, you might start a pressure group to approach the local transport authority on the subject.

Another more immediate solution would be to combine an outing with others who live near you so that you could get into town on a bus and then share a taxi back; or ask a car owner to give you a lift, in exchange for petrol money and perhaps some skill that you can offer.

Taking time to travel

Many people make their retirement the occasion for the 'holiday of a lifetime', now that they have the time to indulge themselves. You can decide when you want to get away from it all and take advantage of low-season prices and bargain breaks. Senior Citizen Railcard holders can obtain concessions on Golden Rail Holidays, brochures for which are available from railway stations or travel agents, and can also purchase a Rail Europe Senior Card from British Rail, which entitles holders to discounts of up to 50 per cent on Continental rail travel.

Fare reductions of up to 40 per cent are offered by British Airways, to senior citizens making mid-week domestic flights, provided there is a minimum stay of six days; and the National Bus Company gives discounts on long-distance buses to pension book holders.

Venturing further afield, you could plan a visit to India, China and the Far East, with a group from the University of the Third Age in association with Saga Holidays, a travel firm which specialises in holidays for the over-60s (address on page 153). Of course, travelling can create a large hole in the budget, but for some couples this is worthwhile. Having made a decision on travel as their retirement hobby, they may have to live very modestly so as to finance their trips overseas. They can gain enormous pleasure from studying the history and culture of the country they are about to visit, and also learning some of the language.

If the informality of a self-catering holiday is more to your taste, Holimarine specialises in this type of holiday for the over 50 age group. Camping and caravanning is a pursuit that attracts people of all ages and walks of life, and the bonus for retired people is that they can travel when the roads are empty of working holidaymakers. Perhaps you would prefer a walking holiday in beautiful surroundings; and, if so, the Country-wide Holiday Association or Holiday Fellowship might be for you. Country-wide have 24 guest houses in Britain and operate holidays on the Continent as well as in the UK (addresses on page 152).

Further reading

Choice (magazine), *Yours* (monthly newspaper),
    Choice Publications, address on page 154

Sex in Later Life
    Ivor Felstein, Granada-Mayflower, 1980

The Joy of Sex
    Alex Comfort, Quartet, 1974

Men and Sex
    Bernie Zilbergeld, Fontana, 1980

The Art of Sensual Massage
    Gordon Inkeles and Murray Todriss, Allen and Unwin, 1982

Women's Experience of Sex
    Sheila Kitzinger, Dorling Kindersley, 1983. Penguin, 1985

Families and How to Survive Them
  Robin Skynner and John Cleese, Methuen, 1983

Passages
  Gail Sheehy, Bantam Books, 1977

Sexual Therapy in the National Marriage Guidance Council
  Jill Heisler, NMGC, reprint 1987, address on page 153

Entitled to Love
  Wendy Greengross, NMGC, 1976

Approaching Retirement
  Consumers' Association, 1983, address on page 154

The Standard Retirement/Briefing File
  Choice Publications Limited, 1985

Some money matters Sue Ward looks at state and employers' pension schemes, taxation and some state benefits

*7*he pension and benefits systems, both state and private, have discriminated heavily against women in the past, seeing us not as people in our own right but as dependants or ex-dependants. In many ways this discrimination has been reduced, but it is still there. Nevertheless, we cannot blame the system altogether, as many people don't think ahead and make the provision they could for a reasonable income in retirement.

This chapter explains how the various pension systems work for women, how you can claim for state benefits you may be entitled to and the major changes relating to pensions and benefits which will take effect from April 1988. In addition, there are some ideas about further changes that should be made to deal with poverty in old age, which is largely a problem for women.

Pensions and benefits from the state

This section explains how the basic pension works and whether it would be better for you to change to paying a full contribution if you don't already do so. It also examines how caring for children or elderly relatives or taking part-time work can affect the level of your pension. In addition, there are the drawbacks you may face if you only receive the basic pension as your husband's dependant.

The section also explains how the basic pension is 'topped up' by the graduated and additional pension, and can be increased by continuing to work after state retirement age. It also covers pensions for widows, divorcees and women who are separated.

When they reach retirement age, most people qualify for the basic pension, which is normally uprated once a year to keep in line with price rises. When earnings rise higher than prices, pensioners therefore *do not* share in the general improvement in the standard of living.

You qualify by paying or being credited with national insurance contributions. Until 1975, for each week during which you earned more than a minimum amount, a stamp went on your national insurance card. In 1975 contributions began to be collected through the PAYE system like income tax, but any you paid before that date still count towards your total. For women, there are two sorts of national insurance contributions: full- and reduced-rate. The reduced-rate does not count for the basic pension.

Calculating your entitlement

To receive the full basic pension, you need a record of full-rate contributions, paid or credited, for about nine-tenths of your 'working life'. For official purposes your working life is between 16 and 60 whether you are actually employed or not during those years. For anyone retiring in the next few years, there are special rules if they were over 16 when the national insurance system began in 1948. If you were paying full stamps before 1948, your working life dates from the year you entered (or re-entered) the state insurance scheme. Your working life can go back as far as April 1936, but not further. The rules protect people who were working before 1936 from losing out, however.

If you came to this country after 1948 as an adult, your working life still started at 16, so you will probably have a reduced pension. However, you may be able to count contributions made elsewhere if that country has a reciprocal Social Security agreement with Britain (DHSS leaflet NP 32 lists these countries). You may also qualify for some pension from the country you left.

Most women retiring in 1987/88 will have 'working lives' of 39 years, and to get a full pension they must have a contribution record for 35 years. For a year to count, you must have paid, or been credited with, contributions on earnings of 52 times the Lower Earnings Limit or more. The Lower Earnings Limit (LEL) is set each year by the government in April, and is roughly the same as the basic pension. If you earn less than this, you do not pay contributions at all; but as soon as you earn more, you pay contributions on all your earnings. A high earner who is paid more than the Upper Earnings Limit (UEL) each week does not pay any more contributions (there are very few women in this position). The UEL is set by the government each year.

For weeks when you signed on as unemployed, or were off sick and receiving statutory sick pay, invalidity benefit, state sickness benefit, or maternity allowance, you get a credit under the NI system. This counts as if you had been earning exactly the amount of the LEL. Sick pay and maternity pay from your employer are dealt with under the PAYE system anyway, so you automatically pay national insurance contributions on them.

At the end of each tax year the DHSS takes the figure for your PAYE earnings and any credits, and calculates whether you have earned or had credits of more than the lower earnings limit. If you have, that year will be a qualifying year towards your pension. You can't use extra national insurance contributions in one year to make up a shortfall in another; each year has to stand on its own. However, in certain limited circumstances you can make voluntary contributions to make up a shortfall in a particular year.

To convert the pre-1975 national insurance stamps to the new system, the DHSS adds up all the stamps paid and credited before 1975, and divides them by 50. It rounds up any years that are left over. This then gives the qualifying years up to April 1975. Under the old system your 'contribution years' differed according to the letter at the end of your national insurance number. However, the conversion of these was done rather arbitrarily, and some people won extra years while others lost.

To find out your contributions record, write to the DHSS local office, giving them your NI number, date of birth, the date you came into the country, where from, and your previous name if you have changed it. Expect to wait two or three months for a reply. At present a 'contribution' or 'qualifying' year runs from April to April.

Paying full-rate contributions

From 1948 when the National Insurance Scheme started, married women were given the option to pay the full-rate contribution for a pension in their own right or to be dependent on their husbands' contributions and to pay a very reduced rate contribution – called the small stamp.

Since 1977 no one starting work or who has had a gap of two complete consecutive tax years in employment has been allowed to pay the small stamp. However, there are many women who are still paying at this rate. They will have to depend on their husbands for their state pension.

If you decide to change over to pay the full-rate contribution, fill in a form, which you can get from the social security office: if you are married, get leaflet NI 1; if you are widowed, leaflet NI 51. Send in the form at any time during the year, but it only takes effect at the beginning of the next tax year, in April.

If you are divorced, you start paying the full rate immediately. If you are a widow and stop receiving benefit because your children have grown up, you must also start paying the full rate, but not until the beginning of the next tax year. If you have a break in employment for two complete consecutive tax years, for whatever reason, you must pay full-rate contributions when you return to work: so, if you leave employment in March 1988, you can return to work at any time up to 5th April 1990 and still pay the reduced rate; but if you wait longer than that, you will have to pay the full rate.

Once you start paying the full rate, you build up benefits in your own right. It takes about 18 months to qualify for the short-term benefits like unemployment and sickness benefit. You can qualify for a reduced retirement pension if you have not paid enough to receive the full pension, but there is a cut-off point. You must pay full stamps for about a quarter of the qualifying years in your working life to get any basic pension at all – even at a reduced rate.

For most women retiring today, a contribution record of 8 years or less means that no pension is paid. If you have paid contributions for, say, 25 years, out of a working life of 39, you would get a pension of 74 per cent of the full amount. This reduction will continue throughout your retirement, so all pension increases will also be reduced. If your pension in your own right is less than the dependent wife's pension, the higher amount will be paid, but the existence of your own pension helps your tax position (see page 72). DHSS leaflet NP 32 explains how much you will get.

Changing over to the full rate?

Many women have now moved voluntarily to paying the full national insurance contribution. It is worth thinking about, because if you are on a wage of less than £60 a week, the difference in cost between paying 3.85 per cent and 5 per cent of your earnings is not very great. Consider the following factors in deciding whether to pay full-rate contributions:

- Can you build up enough pension, when you retire, to take you above the rate of the dependent wife's pension, which is 60 per cent of the full pension?

- Are you retiring before your husband does? You will have to wait until he starts drawing his pension before getting yours, if you are his 'dependant'.

- If you are going to be away from work for a period in the future, you will have to pay the full rate when you return to paid employment, so it might be as well to start now, and build up the maximum benefit.

As a general rule, the younger you are, the more likely you are to benefit from changing over to the full rate. If you are over 45 or 50, you are unlikely to find it worthwhile, unless you had a considerable period of paying full contributions before you got married. If you are about to take a break in paid employment, and know this will be longer than two years, it is always worth 'electing' to pay the full rate before you leave your current job. It won't make any difference immediately, but it will have a considerable impact in the long run, as explained in the next section.

Home responsibilities protection

Many women spend some years away from paid employment bringing up children or looking after elderly or disabled relatives. Before 6th April 1978, this created a gap in their contribution record and penalised them in retirement. Since that date, though, the Home Responsibilities Protection scheme has given credits for years spent away from regular paid work.

To qualify, you must be paying, or have told the DHSS you intend to pay, national insurance contributions at the full rate. You must also build up, through your whole working life at least 20 years' national insurance contributions, though the years need not be consecutive. When you retire, the DHSS looks at the gaps in your record for full tax years when you were receiving child benefit or a benefit for caring for an invalid. These years will not count as part of your working life, and the number of qualifying years you need for a full pension will be reduced.

For someone receiving child benefit, or supplementary benefit (income support from April 1988) to look after a sick or disabled person, home responsibilities protection is automatic. However, you must claim HRP if you are looking after someone who is receiving an attendance allowance or constant attendance allowance, using the form attached to DHSS leaflet NP 27.

Home responsibilities protection only counts for full tax years, which is a disadvantage, since most of us do not arrange our lives from April to April. If you are returning to work after child or relative care, try to ensure that you can earn enough in the remainder of that tax year to take you above the lower earnings limit.

Part-time work and your pension

Anyone who earns below the lower earnings limit does not pay national insurance contributions, and builds up no record within the national insurance system. If you earn more than the LEL, you pay contributions on all earnings – a big disincentive to raising your hours, and therefore your pay, by that small amount. About half of all part-timers earn below the limit, and therefore do not exist for national insurance purposes.

If you are working fewer than 15 hours a week, you also have very few employment rights, until you have been in the same job for at least 5 years, working at least 8 hours a week. So if the offer is made to you to work shorter hours, think carefully about these aspects, and what it will do to your pension.

Dependent wife's pension

By the turn of the century, the majority of women will probably be entitled to the basic pension in their own right, though perhaps not at the full amount. Currently, though, many women are dependent on their husbands' pensions.

If you are married without a pension in your own right and are treated as your husband's dependant, then he draws an extra pension for you. If you could qualify either for a reduced pension of your own or a dependant's addition, the higher of the two would be paid. However, the addition cannot be drawn until your husband retires, and if he works on after this age, you will have to wait to receive this pension.

Even if your pension in your own right is fairly small, it may be worth claiming for any years after you reach 60 before your husband retires. You can get a wife's earned income tax relief on the part of your pension which you earned from your own contributions.

Graduated pension

This pension existed between 1961 and April 1975. It was not properly inflation proofed, but anyone who paid national insurance contributions, even at the reduced rate, during that period will have a right to some graduated pension, however small, or to an equivalent amount from an employer's scheme. The graduated scheme gave worse value to women than to men, on the grounds that we retire earlier and live longer. Graduated pension is increased annually in the same way as the basic pension.

If you are married and not entitled to a basic pension on your own contributions, you can still claim the graduated pension, even if your husband has not yet retired. If it is less than £1.05 a week, it will be paid as a lump sum once a year. Claiming can make a difference, though, to your husband's position if he is postponing retirement, as explained in DHSS leaflet NI 92.

Many employers 'contracted out' of the Graduated Pension Scheme and agreed to pay at least the same amount as their employees would have received from the State under the graduated scheme, from their own occupational scheme. However, many employers arranged after April 1975 to buy people back into the graduated scheme. You should have been notified by your employer if he opted for this but if you never heard anything, or cannot remember, write to that employer, or to the DHSS, and enquire.

Additional pension

This started in 1978 and is commonly known as SERPS. The initials stand for the State Earnings Related Pension Scheme. Anyone who earns enough to pay national insurance contributions is either 'contracted-in' to SERPS or 'contracted-out' because they belong to either an employer's scheme or a personal pension scheme. After January 1988, there will be a third option of 'contracting-out' with a personal pension.

In practice, most people, however good or bad their employer's scheme, will be contracted out for some part of their working lives. The formula for calculating how much additional pension based on your earnings you should get is fairly complicated, and the present formula will change in the future.

People who are self-employed are not included in SERPS and

can therefore only provide for their retirement with a personal pension plan plus the basic state pension.

In order to calculate what your entitlement to the additonal pension is, the DHSS starts by assuming that you have always been contracted in. Your earnings above the LEL and below the UEL are assessed for each year since 1978 when the scheme started. Then they are recalculated to take account of the increase in national average earnings between the date you earned the money and your retirement. Then you are paid 1/80th of the average of all those years' earnings, for every year you've been in the scheme.

Once the scheme has been running for 20 years or more, claimants will not build up any more 80ths. The maximum claimants can get is 20/80ths (one-quarter) of your revalued average earnings. After 1998, these figures start being 'phased down' by $\frac{1}{2}$ per cent a year, so that anyone retiring after the year 2008 gets only 20 per cent (one fifth) of their relevant earnings, after they have been revalued and averaged over the whole of the working life. Years when you are at home and getting home responsiblities protection will not be counted, but years when you are unemployed or working part-time will, and will bring down the average, so you will end up with a lower pension.

If you were contracted out for part of your working life, the DHSS tells your employer how much to pay as pension. This must override any scheme rules which would give you a worse deal. How much the employer pays depends on how long you were in that scheme. A woman who has been in an employer's scheme for 17 years out of a total working life of 34 years will expect her employer to pay exactly half of her additional pension. This amount is called the Guaranteed Minimum Pension, or GMP for short.

After retirement, the additional pension increases in line with prices, like the basic pension. Employers do not have to provide this inflation-proofing of the GMP, at present. The state assumes that they are not doing so and gives increases on all of the additional pension as if you had never been contracted out. After April 1988, they will have to increase GMP built up in future years by 3 per cent a year, once it starts being paid. The state will then increase the additional pension by its own inflation-proofing minus that amount.

Moving from job to job makes no difference to the additional pension. Depending on how long you are with a particular employer, the GMP can be bought back into the state scheme, preserved, and to some extent be inflation-proofed, or transferred to a new employer. The preserved GMP can sometimes fall short of what you would have had from SERPS, and in these cases the state makes up the difference.

If you will reach the age of 60 before 1998, you can work out very roughly what your SERPS will be in a series of steps:

- Take an average figure for your total weekly PAYE earnings this year.
- If the earnings figure is higher than the upper earnings limit, take that as the figure.
- Deduct the lower earnings limit, and divide the resulting figure by 80.
- If you were aged 40 or more in 1978, multiply by the number of years before you will be 60, the state retirement age. If you were younger than 40 in 1978, multiply by 20.

The figure you get from those calculations will give you a rough idea of the pension you would receive if there were no inflation nor pay rises between now and your retirement date. In fact, as your salary increases so will your pension.

Deferring retirement

If you want to carry on working after you are 60, you have the choice of drawing your state pension and adding your earnings to it, or postponing your retirement. You no longer pay national insurance contributions on your earnings, and the DHSS will tell your employer that they should no longer be deducted.

If you draw your pension, you can earn up to a certain amount a week without affecting it. Above this level, however, there is an Earnings Rule, which means that for earnings over a certain amount, a percentage will be deducted until you won't receive any pension at all. Whatever you earn, will be taxed. For this purpose the state pension and your earnings are added together, but the tax is deducted from your earnings.

There is a similar earnings rule for the dependent wife's pension, and for this purpose an occupational pension also counts as earnings if the wife is under 60. A widow can earn any amount without losing her widow's pension, although this is taxed.

If you want to defer your retirement for up to five years, you receive increments (increases) on the pension. If you wait the full five years, the pension will be one-third higher than what you would have received at age 60. If you have a reduced level of benefit because you have paid too few contributions, carrying on working is one way of improving your pension.

However, you do not receive an increment for any week when you or a dependant are receiving another national insurance benefit. So a widow who defers retirement and carries on drawing the widow's allowance gets no increase in her pension. If you become unemployed, you draw unemployment benefit at the same rate as retirement pension, but there is no increment for those weeks.

Deciding whether to defer retirement or not depends on the level of your earnings and the pension you would get. You can cancel retirement only once, and you can tell the DHSS at any time that you would like to retire immediately.

After November 1987, a woman who wants to carry on working after state retirement age will be protected from unfair dismissal by her employer, provided the retirement age for a man doing her job is above the age of 60. She won't, though, be protected from being made redundant, and her redundancy payments may be reduced if she is over 60. This change in the law was forced on the government by the European Court of Justice which decided in favour of a woman who did not want to retire at 60.

Claiming your pension

About four months before your 60th birthday, the DHSS should send you a form to claim your pension. If you haven't been informed three months before your birthday, write to them. Fill in and return the claim form as soon as you get it, even if you intend to continue working; there is space on the form to say this is what you're doing. If you delay claiming for more than three months, you cannot normally get the pension backdated.

When you are eligible to claim your pension, you will receive a letter from your local social security office saying how much pension you will get. If you think it is the wrong amount, you have a right of appeal, within three months of being told the amount to an independent Social Security Appeal Tribunal. Get advice from your local Citizen's Advice Bureau, trade union, or a welfare rights advice office.

All the different parts of the state pension will come on one order book; you cash this weekly at the post office. Pensions are paid a week in advance, and for anyone who retired after September 1984, the payday is now a Monday. It's best to finish work on a Friday because you can't get pension for any day of retirement that comes before your first payday.

You can have your pension paid direct into a bank, building society, or National Giro account. It will then be paid four-weekly or quarterly in arrears. Leaflet NI 105 explains in detail how to go about this.

If you are going abroad for less than three months, you can cash all your pension orders when you come home. But a pension order cannot be cashed more than three months after the date printed on it. If you are going abroad for three months or more, tell your local social security office well in advance. Your pension can then normally be paid into a bank in the United Kingdom or to someone else authorised by you.

If you go abroad to live, or remain outside the UK for three months or more, you can continue to receive the pension, but you *may not* get any increase when the pension goes up. However, if you live in a Common Market country or in one of the other countries with special arrangements, increases can be paid. For details contact either your local social security office or the DHSS at the address on page 154.

Widows pensions and benefits

Because the state assumes that women are men's natural dependants, widows benefits are reasonably generous, whereas widowers are expected to be earning or receiving some form of social security in their own right.

Until April 1988, as a widow under 60 you are entitled to the widow's allowance for the first 26 weeks after your husband's death provided he paid enough contributions. To get this allowance, fill in the form at the back of the special death certificate you'll be given when you register the death. Send the form to your local social security office, and you'll be sent claim form BW 1 to be completed in order to receive the book of orders to cash in for the widow's allowance.

After the first 26 weeks, you may be entitled to the widowed mother's allowance if you have dependent children. When you no longer have children dependent on you – and provided you are between the ages of 40 and 60 – you are eligible for a widow's pension. Leaflet N1 196 gives the age related rates for this.

From April 1988 the widow's allowance will be abolished. Instead the widow's pension or widowed mother's allowance will be payable immediately on the husband's death. A young childless widow who does not qualify for either of these benefits will no longer be entitled to the weekly national insurance benefit even for the first 26 weeks. A lump sum widow's payment of £1,000 will be paid if you would have qualified for the widow's allowance. Eligibility for the widow's pension will be reduced to those between the ages of 45 and 60.

When you retire, you will get the basic pension instead of the widow's pension you were getting. Depending on your contributions record, you may get more money from the basic pension. If you want to continue working until 65, you can choose between the widow's or the basic pension.

If you are over 60 when you become widowed, you are entitled to the basic pension, based on your own contributions, your husband's or, if necessary, a mixture of both. You will also receive half your husband's graduated pension and all of his additional pension if he contributed to SERPS, so long as this would not take your pension above the maximum you could have had if you had been earning at the upper earnings limit throughout. If his employer's scheme has 'contracted out', they must pay you half his guaranteed minimum pension, and the state makes up the difference.

In order to qualify for these national insurance benefits, you must have been married to your husband on the date he died. If you were separated at the time, you are still treated as a dependant. If your husband had more than one wife, under the laws of another country, then only his first wife receives a widow's pension. However, if you as a widow subsequently 'live with a man as his wife', you can lose your entitlement to the widow's pension without benefit of marriage lines!

Divorce and separation

If you are over 60 and drawing a full pension in your own right, this will not be affected by divorce. If you have made too few contributions to qualify for the basic pension, you may be able to use some of your ex-husband's contribution record to build up your pension to the full amount. However, if you remarry before you are 60, you cannot claim a pension on your first husband's contributions. If you should divorce for a second time, you can claim on your second husband's contribution record only.

Claiming on an ex-husband's contributions is a matter of book-keeping and doesn't reduce his pension, and can be done confidentially. Though the system is quite helpful to divorcees, it does involve the assumption that women are a piece of property being passed from one man to another!

If you are separated, you can be worse off if you do not have a full pension in your own right. You only receive the lower dependent wife's pension and can only claim on your husband's contributions after he draws a pension.

Means-tested benefits

Many women need extra financial help from the state in order to bring their incomes up to a minimum figure and to help with their rent and rates. You can apply for help through the supplementary pension (income support after April 1988) and housing benefit systems. As these systems are changing considerably in April 1988, this section explains the current regulations first and then the new ones.

What you get from means-tested benefits depends on what your income is. For many older people this brings back memories of the means test in the thirties, when the visiting officer would tell you to sell the piano before you could receive any payments. This is one reason why over one million pensioners who would be entitled to supplementary pension are not claiming, although the benefits are a right, not a charity, and we all pay for them through our taxes.

Supplementary pension is complicated, and to understand how it applies to you and the latest rates of payment, see the leaflets and books listed on pages 79-80. Supplementary pension tops up your income to the level the government thinks you need. The minimum figure is called the 'scale rate' which is supplemented by certain weekly additions depending on your age, health and other circumstances. At present, if you have savings of over £3,000, you are not entitled to claim.

If you live with a 'grown-up' child or children, you have a right to claim for yourself; but if you are not a separate householder, your benefit will be at a lower rate. On the other hand, if you, as a pensioner, are the householder and have relatives living with you, you'll receive the higher rate of benefit. It can sometimes be difficult to establish who is the householder in a particular case. If the DHSS gets this, or anything else, wrong when assessing, you have a right of appeal to an independent tribunal.

From April 1988 the supplementary pension system will cease to exist and will be replaced by income support. Under this there will be a basic personal allowance topped up by premiums for certain groups. For elderly people this will be on two levels – a premium for people aged 60 to 79, and a higher rate for those who are 80 and over or for younger pensioners who are sick or disabled. Weekly additional payments will no longer be available, and there will be no special householder rate. The savings limit will be raised from £3,000 to £6,000 with scaled deductions between these figures.

As the supplementary pension scale rates do not cover rent or general rates, help with these comes from the council as housing benefit. At present there is no limit on the amount of capital you can have when claiming this, but from April 1988 there will be the same savings limit as for income support. You can qualify for housing benefit on a higher income than for supplementary benefit. The amount you receive depends on your income and the level of rent and rates you pay. It could cover all your rate payment, but after April 1988, anyone in receipt of income support and housing benefit will have to pay 20 per cent of their rates.

If you're receiving supplementary pension, the social security office should inform the council that you also need housing benefit, and they should work it out and notify you. It may be as well to remind them, though. If you're not receiving supplementary pension, you have to claim yourself from the council. Ask at the town hall, local advice centre, or the local housing office.

The golden rule with these benefits is if in doubt, claim; and read *Your Rights*, also published by Age Concern. The Citizen's Advice Bureau, a council welfare rights officer, or a neighbourhood advice centre should be able to advise about your individual circumstances; but you have nothing to lose by filling in the form. To apply for supplementary pension get leaflet SB 1 from the post office, fill in your name and address, sign it and send it off in the pre-paid envelope. The DHSS may then send you a more detailed form to fill in and return. If you want to deal with the issue face to face, ask for an appointment, either in the local office or for an officer to visit you in your home.

How pensions are taxed

State pensions are considered as earned income for tax purposes; but there is a special age allowance when one member of a couple is over 65, (higher if you are over 80) so you won't be taxed if the state pension is your only income.

A dependent wife's pension is included in her husband's income and is offset against the married man's tax allowance. A pension in your own right is automatically offset against the wife's earned income allowance. If you wish to confirm this, write to your tax office, and read the relevant leaflets and books listed on page 80.

If you are not paying tax, think about where your savings are. Building society and bank deposit accounts are taxed at source, so you are losing money if your savings are there. But National Savings accounts are not taxed at source, and you are allowed £70 a year tax-free interest.

Improving pensions and benefits

Instead of accepting the government's reforms of pensions and benefits, which are mainly designed to save it money, women should be campaigning for changes in the system to give pensioners more money, as the problem of poverty in old age mainly affects women – with three quarters of those people relying on supplementary benefit being female. Some much needed pension and benefit reforms would be:

- Remove or reduce the contribution conditions that exclude people from obtaining a full pension.
- Credit existing pensioners into SERPS.
- Backdate home responsibilities protection to cover women coming up to retirement now.

It is surely the mark of a civilised society to treat its elderly members well. Where would we be but for the work done by previous generations?

Pensions from your employer

Many people belong to a pension scheme run by an employer. This is usually called an occupational or company pension if the employer is private; and in the public sector it is often known as superannuation. This section discusses these pensions, how they can be increased by additional voluntary contributions, how you can build up a pension if you have no access to an employer's scheme and how divorce affects your right to your ex-husband's pension. In 1988 there is to be a new system of personal pensions, explained on page 76.

Most occupational schemes pay a proportion of your earnings when you retire and are called final earnings schemes. How much you get depends on how long you have worked for the employer and the accrued rate at which the pension builds up. For tax purposes, your state pension will be added to your occupational one, and any tax due will be deducted from the latter.

The most common rates for building up a pension are 1/80th of earnings for each year you have been in the scheme, or 1/60th. These fractions are based on the idea that you will work for 40 years, and therefore end up with either half, or two-thirds, of your earnings at retirement. As most women – and indeed, most men – do not stay 40 years with one employer, they usually receive less than this.

Since 1975, pension schemes have been required by law to give equal access to men and women, but not equal benefits; and the requlations of the scheme must not discriminate directly against an employee's age or length of service needed to qualify for joining. However, schemes can discriminate indirectly – for instance, by admitting personal assistants but not secretaries, and full-timers but not part-time employees – and many do. Both the Sex Discrimination and Equal Pay Acts excluded pensions schemes from their scope, but EEC legislation may eventually change this.

Most employers' schemes are 'contracted out' of SERPS which means that the employer has agreed to provide at least as much from his scheme as you would receive from SERPS. In return for giving this quarantee, both employer and employee pay lower national insurance contributions, and the money goes instead into a separate pension fund. Contributions to an occupational scheme are eligible for full tax relief on up to 15 per cent of earnings whether or not the scheme is contracted out.

There are considerable differences between schemes in various public services (the NHS, local government, the civil service) and private company schemes.

Public service superannuation

Two-thirds of women working in the public services are members of a scheme, and joining is generally a condition of employment. There is discrimination however against people working part time, for instance, in the universities; and only since April 1986 have part-timers in local government been able to join. They now have the opportunity to 'buy back' service, which is often worthwhile.

The pension in these schemes is generally based on 1/80th of your earnings for the last few years before retirement, plus a lump sum of 3/80ths of the same earnings. So if you have been in the scheme all your life, you would have a half pension and a lump sum – which is tax free – of $1\frac{1}{2}$ times your earnings. This pension increases in line with the rise in prices. If you leave after less than 5 years in the scheme (2 years after April 1988), you can have a refund of your contributions, with a deduction to buy you back into the State scheme and to pay the tax you have previously not paid. If you had more than 5 years' service before leaving (2 years after April 1988), you will be given a 'deferred pension', which is inflation proofed.

Pension transfers between different parts of the public sector are easy, so that if you stop being a teacher and become a civil servant, for instance, you get full credit in the new scheme. Transferring into the private sector is more difficult. The ease of transferring from one public service scheme to another and the fact that your pension keeps up with price increases are important factors to consider when comparing them with private sector schemes, which generally do not keep up with inflation and where you can lose out if you leave.

If you die before retirement, there is a lump sum payable, usually to your estate, and also a widow's pension. A widower's pension as a right used to be very rare in the public sector, although the civil service has now introduced one. Some nationalised industries already offer these benefits; and in some cases, such as the teachers' scheme, a woman with a dependent husband can arrange for him to receive a pension on her death.

Dependent children are not usually covered by superannuation, although you should notify your employer if you are the sole breadwinner. Many public sector employers do not bother to tell single parents about their rights in this situation, so ask your personnel or payroll department what your dependants will receive on your death. Some schemes allow you to give up part of your pension for cohabitees or other adult dependants, and this could also be worth checking on.

Company schemes

These follow a rather different pattern and generally exclude part-timers. They often pay a higher pension, based on 1/60th for each year of service rather than 1/80th, but the tax-free lump sum has to be bought by giving up part of your pension. Usually, for every £1 of annual pension you give up at 60, you will receive a lump sum of £11. An increase in the pension, though, may well only be based on the amount you have left.

The lump sum paid on your death in service can be as much as four times your earnings, and is usually paid at the discretion of the scheme trustees. You have the opportunity in most schemes to make your wishes known by filling in a form or sending a letter to the trustees. Anyone whose family circumstances are at all unusual should do so.

Company schemes generally provide widows' pensions as of right. Widowers' pensions are less common, but are spreading. Often a widower has to prove that he was dependent on his wife before he can receive benefit. This discrimination is based simply on prejudice, because the cost of providing a widower's pension is very small. After April 1988, company schemes will have to begin building up a small widower's pension for contracted out membership from that date onwards. There is nothing to stop them doing better than this and backdating this improvement.

If you die within five years of retirement, most schemes pay the balance of the five years' pension as a lump sum. If death occurs after that period, the scheme may pay a funeral benefit, but the widow goes straight on to the widow's pension.

Increasing your pension

In many schemes, you're allowed to pay additional voluntary contributions (AVCs) to buy a bigger pension. You can pay up to 15 per cent of your earnings altogether as contributions and still get tax relief. In public sector schemes, you can buy 'added years', which are fully inflation proofed. In the private sector, what you get will depend on how well the AVCs are invested. You'll often be able to turn the pension your contributions have brought into a bigger tax-free lump sump. AVCs are a very efficient way of saving, especially if you have only a few years to go before you retire.

Ask the personnel department about an AVC scheme. All companies must have one after April 1988. If you do not like the look of the one linked to your scheme, you will have the right to buy a 'free-standing' one from any provider; but take care to study the small print in the contract.

Personal pensions

After January 1988 there will also be a new sort of scheme, a personal pension (PP). This will have two sub-divisions, a contracted out part which will replace SERPS, and an ordinary PP which can go on top of SERPS or of the contracted out part. Personal pensions work on a different principle from most ocupational schemes or superannuation. Instead of being based on your earnings, they depend on what contributions you make, how much these earn in dividends and interest payments, and what annuity you can buy when you retire. This principle is called 'money purchase' or 'defined contributions'.

If you opt for the minimum, contracted out personal pension, you will pay the full-rate of national insurance contributions, and the government will pass on a rebate to the firm providing the pension (a bank, a building society, an insurance company, or a unit trust). For the first six years, it will give an additional 2 per cent if you were not contracted out of SERPS already. This minimum contribution can only go to buy a pension at retirement date and a dependant wife's pension, not a lump sum or the chance to retire early.

A woman retiring at 60 will get a lower pension from a PP than a man would at 65, even if she has paid in the same amount over the same number of years. This pension replaces your SERPS; and the DHSS will assume that you are receiving at least as much as you would have been from them (you might be, but you might receive much less – there are no guarantees).

If you want any other benefits, or if you want to stay in SERPS but build on top of it, you will have to pay extra, and make your own arrangements. This could then go to buy you a bigger pension, or a death benefit, or an earlier retirement date.

After April 1988, you will have the right to leave your employer's scheme as well, or not join one when you start a new job, and take out a PP.

Because of the way PPs are structured, they may well give a better pension than SERPS does if you pay in when you are young; but the older you are, the less value they are. The experts say that for a woman over about 40, SERPS is definitely going to be better, and if she has been paying into a contracted out PP scheme up to that time, she should change over then. PPs at the basic level are unlikely to beat even a moderately good occupational pension scheme, and anyone in a good scheme – especially if it is inflation proofed like those in the public services – would be unwise to move out. It is important to bear in mind these factors:

• There is no guarantee on PPs – you could do better, but if inflation went up, or the stock market turned sour, or the people you were buying it from were not very clever, you could do very much worse.

• The people selling PPs will be aiming to make a profit – both the organisation providing them, and the broker or sales representative doing the selling. Its estimated that about 20 per cent of your total contributions to the average insurance company scheme go towards expenses. Of these, up to three quarters of your contributions in the first year will go as commission to the broker or sales representative.

• Though the insurance companies make promises of very high investment returns, the small print will make clear that these are not guaranteed. Check the past investment record as well as the promises. And remember that the benefits won't usually change with inflation – so a figure that looks more like a telephone number now than a pension may be much smaller, in real terms, when you retire.

Widows and personal pension schemes

If someone has taken out a PP which is contracted out of SERPS, the widow's pension under SERPS or under the occupational pension scheme to which she belonged previously will be replaced by an annuity bought out of the fund of contributions built up so far. For the widow of a younger man or of one who has not been paying into a personal pension scheme for very long, this could be a very small amount – perhaps only a few hundred pounds a year. So if a husband is considering taking out a PP, he should certainly discuss the terms with his wife so that they both understand what is being given up.

There is also a widower's pension from a PP, but again this will be very small.

Divorce and employers' schemes

Usually, you lose the widow's pension at the time of a divorce, though you may be able to benefit from the lump sum payment on death. In some cases, it's possible for the scheme trustees to split the widow's pension between both wives, if the man was paying maintenance to his ex-wife; but the pension is often not big enough to make this worthwhile.

Solicitors are supposed to take account, when working out a financial settlement on divorce, of the value of the lost occupational pension rights for a dependent wife. But they often forget, or the matter gets overlooked in the settlement; and consequently many women lose both widow's pension and life assurance. If this happens, to recoup the loss, try to pay as much as you can in AVCs into your occupational scheme or a separate one, or into a personal pension scheme – if necessary right up to the tax limit.

Further reading

Your Rights 1987
  Age Concern England, updated annually

Your Taxes and Savings 1987/88
  Age Concern England, updated annually

Disability Rights Handbook
  Disability Alliance, 1987, address on page 146

Rights Guide to Non-Means-Tested Benefits;
National Welfare Benefits Handbook
  Child Poverty Action Group, address on page 153

What Will My Pension Be?
  Consumers Association/ Hodder and Stoughton, 1985

Money Guide for Women
  Nigel Smith and Jill Greatorex, Coronet Books, 1986

DHSS Leaflets

Divorced   NI 95
Earning Extra Pension by Cancelling Your Retirement   NI 92
How to Appeal   NI 246
Living Together as Husband and Wife   NI 247
Looking After Someone at Home (Home Responsibilities
Protection)   NI 27
Made Redundant?   NI 231
Mobility Allowance   NI 211, NI 243
New Ways of Claiming for Couples   NI 248
National Insurance Guide for Widows   NI 51
Part-Time work and Social Security Benefits   NI 242
Payment Direct into Bank or Building Society Account   NI 105
Retiring? Your Pension and other Benefits   FB 6
Retirement Benefits for Married Women   NP 32B
Retirement Pension   NP 32
Supplementary Benefit leaflets   SB 1, SB 8, SB 16, SB 17, SB 18,
SB 19, SB 21

Inland Revenue leaflets

Other government leaflets

Caring for others

Christine Orton discusses how to manage the role of carer

*I*n the years leading up to retirement and after, women often find themselves in the role of carer, looking after an aged partner or ailing parents and other relations, or in certain situations, adult children. It is a task which brings both pleasure and pain. It can be hard physically as well as emotionally to be caring for someone who is ill and dependent, especially when we are growing older ourselves. But it can also give deep satisfaction to have this opportunity of showing love and concern for someone who is close and who has probably shown the same care for us.

Mary and Jim are typical of many couples in this situation. They had retired from work within a year of each other and were looking forward to spending time together doing many of the things that bringing up children and working had so far prevented.

Then Mary's mother died, and her father was left on his own. At first he coped well and went on living independently in his own home. But a stroke left him paralysed, and after a spell in hospital he moved in with his daughter and son-in-law. Caring for him became an almost full-time job because he could do so little for himself; and it was difficult for Mary and Jim to go out together, especially as her father grew less able to get around, and he needed a great deal of help at home.

Even though caring meant postponing many of the plans Mary and Jim had for their retirement, when her father died, Mary expressed satisfaction about the time spent caring for him. 'It brought us very close as a family, and we were able to make the end of his life as peaceful and comfortable as possible. There were moments of course, when Jim and I felt desperately tired and even resentful because there was so much work involved. But there were also some very happy and amusing times, and I'm so thankful now that we had the experience.'

Mary and Jim learned two important rules about caring. The first is to share the role as much as possible with those close to the person who is dependent, drawing on all possible sources of help outside the home (detailed later in this chapter). The other is to be as organised as possible. Looking after a frail and elderly person is very much a management task. Thinking about it carefully in a practical way rather than just muddling through makes a great deal of difference in coping successfully day by day.

Preparing to care

For some who have been caring for a dependent relative for many years the problems involved are only too familiar. For others this will be a new situation, but one which needs to be taken into consideration when planning for retirement. As with everything else, being aware of the possibilities and preparing for them are essential. A sudden emergency may make a situation far more complicated to deal with if no plan of action has been previously thought over.

It may seem pessimistic, even morbid, to think about a child, parents, a partner or ourselves becoming more and more dependent as the years go by. In fact, it is simply realistic, since this happens for so many people. To decide, for instance, *who* will do the caring and *where* gives everyone, including the older person, a chance to make their wishes known. Some of the reasons for the caring so often falling on the shoulders of a woman may be unavoidable. But to automatically assume that this is the woman's role when other choices are available or when the task can be shared isn't fair and is certainly a point of discussion.

Where the caring takes place will often decide who does the bulk of the task anyway, and this is a crucial decision which needs talking about well in advance, particularly where ageing parents are concerned. Whether they remain in their own homes, move to a new one nearer relatives or close friends, move in with sons or daughters, or into sheltered or residential accommodation — all need to be considered.

Some older people dread the idea of moving out of their own homes, while others would enjoy being near or actually living with their relatives. In the same way, it helps if partners can talk over these possibilities for their own later years, or for those of a dependent child.

Establishing 'house rules'

People who have had experience of caring for someone on a long-term basis stress how important it is to lay down certain 'house rules' beforehand. This would include agreeing to set holiday breaks each year when other relatives and friends or an outside helping agency can take over, so that the carers get a much needed break. One social worker who had cared for her own mother for many years explains below how important it is to take on the role of carer for the right reasons:

《 *It shouldn't be simply out of guilt or duty — if you already have a good relationship it helps such a lot. You also need a reasonably good sized house. If a home hasn't got much space and there are still children around, the chances of it working without conflict are reduced.*

'It's also very necessary to retain independence on both sides. The older person should be treated with respect and should feel free to keep up with friends and have them home. Similarly the rest of the family must have separate interests and lives, even some meals apart if need be.

'Before taking any decisions about living together, everyone should agree on the basic structure and routine of how it can work, from sharing the bathroom and kitchen to how to manage finances. 》

She also points out the importance of the older person having some privacy however dependent he or she becomes, with a room that can double as a sitting room and includes, if possible, TV, electric kettle, cups, and so on, so that there is an independent place to be.

Who cares for the carers?

There are many reasons why an increasing number of people, men as well as women, find themselves in the role of home nurse nowadays. Medical know-how means that people are living longer anyway, though not necessarily in the best of health.

At the same time, the new accent on 'community care' means that elderly people and disabled children who have reached a certain level of dependency and inability to cope – and who would once have gone into hospital or residential care – are now encouraged to remain at home. It is of course necessary for someone to look after them in the home, and though there are some back-up services available, the responsibility mainly falls on one person – usually a close relative or friend, usually a woman.

For many, this would be the natural choice anyway with or without government policy, and it is generally agreed that the ideals behind community care are good ones. Most of us would prefer when ill or very elderly to be looked after by those we know and love rather than taken to a strange and unfamiliar place.

But a balance has to be kept, and it is important that the quality of the carer's life is borne in mind as well as the quality of life for the one who is being cared for. The pleasures and rewards of looking after a loved one can be immense. But for many people, especially as they grow older themselves, and especially if the professional support is not there, the burden can become intolerable. As emphasised in an Equal Opportunities Commission report, just because people are doing a good job which they may have chosen to do, does not mean they should be ignored and left to cope alone:

« *Despite the social and economic restrictions experienced by carers, there is no doubt that for many people the emotional rewards of caring far outweigh the disadvantages. However, the existance of intangible advantages does not justify the continuation of policies which ignore the basic rights of women who want to play a full and active part in society. The rewards of caring are more likely to be forthcoming when the caring role is freely chosen by the carer, and she is welcomed by her charge.* »

According to another organisation working in this field, the National Council for Carers and their Elderly Dependents (address on page 146), not enough professionals recognise these rights and needs, or encourage carers to do so. Indeed, many carers don't identify themselves as such, partly because this particular job description has been coined on their behalf and many don't even know what it means:

« *Also it's a role that tends to creep up on people – you don't suddenly wake up one morning and find you are a carer. It tends to happen gradually over a period of time. But it is important for people to understand that this is a job they are doing, and for both they and the professionals involved to realise its significance. There must be an even balance between rights and responsibilities.* »

Different caring relationships

People facing retirement might find themselves responsible for the care of others for a number of different reasons. As already discussed in the chapter 'Retiring on your own' there are women who in the real sense have never left home, but have spent all their spare time outside work living with, and later looking after, their parents. Some may have taken part-time jobs so that they could cope with the increasing demands at home, some may never have worked at all outside the home.

The majority of women, however, will probably have left parents and home a long time before, and spent many of their subsequent years caring for children and a partner, running the home and having a job too. Then, when the children at least are independent, life comes full circle, and ageing or ill parents and other relatives need their attention. Many daughters – and sons too – faced with this need make incredible sacrifices in their own lives to make sure that this is done well. The time and effort demanded of them may put a strain on their relationship with a partner, who may have been looking forward to the years when they could be alone again as a couple.

It may of course be a partner who is the one who needs caring for. Because men more commonly become ill and die before women, it is the wife who is most likely to become unofficial nurse.

Betty and George had both worked and were able to enjoy a few years of their retirement together before he had a major stroke. Betty now in her late 60s, spends all her time looking after him, helping him dress, wash and go to the toilet.

Their life completely changed the day George had his stroke. Even though they were retired, they had been leading a very active life. He had been doing voluntary work for young people, and they used to enjoy going dancing and out to a club for a drink on Saturday nights. As Betty summed up the situation: 'It is just the two of us at home alone. He's been so good about it and I love being with him. But I do get tired with all the fetching and carrying'.

For some women there are both parents and a partner to care for, making their day revolve around caring.

Jill is 60, and, since she retired early from her job as a dinner lady, has been caring full-time for her 90-year-old bedridden mother and for her husband who has Parkinson's disease. Jill's life revolves round them both, and there have been times when she has even had difficulty getting to the shops, let alone keeping up her own interests and going out in the evenings. She is cheerful and stoical like so many others in her position, but to any outsider it seems like a hard life.

For another section of women, childcare never comes to an end even when the children have become adults. Children with a very severe mental or physical handicap can spend some of their time at special schools or residential centres, but once they reach adulthood facilities are often no longer available. The large part of the responsibility falls back on the parents – or, in some cases, on grandparents.

Gladys who is 68 and has angina and problems with her legs spends all her time looking after her mentally handicapped grand-daughter who also suffers from epilepsy.

Luckily in all three of the situations outlined above, the carers have eventually discovered that support for them is available and this has made a great deal of difference to their lives. Betty and George found their support in the local day centre, Jill from a relative's support group and Gladys through a care attendant scheme that relieved her responsibilities for a few hours each day.

Women, the forgotten army

The fact that it is women rather than men who are commonly the carers won't come as a surprise to most people. Indeed, it is often assumed that women are the 'natural' carers, and that such work isn't quite suitable for a man. From motherhood onwards, women are automatically slotted into the role of nurturing and tending to the needs of others. Another study reported by the Equal Opportunities Commission (address on page 146) in their book *Carers and Services*, which compares the situation of men and women looking after dependent elderly relations, shows that 59 per cent of all carers are women.

> « *In a society where norms, attitudes, expectations and behaviour are strongly influenced by gender, it is predictable that the experience of caring will be different for men and women carers. The situation is further complicated because of the tensions created by conflicting expectations. Thus, for example, a woman's wish to work outside the home might conflict with the expectation that she should care for an elderly relative. Conversely, a man's wish to care for an elderly relative might conflict with the expectation that he should go out to work.* »

After retirement these expectations may no longer even be relevant, yet habits die hard and probably patterns of caring have already been established which will go on exerting an influence even though there is no longer any need.

There are other reasons for the predominance of women carers, even after retirement. As already pointed out, men on average, become ill and die sooner than women, so there are more women forced by circumstances into being carers. Yet another influence is less obvious. Because women live longer, they make up the majority of the very elderly population requiring care, and they in turn look to their daughters and other female relatives.

Studies have also shown that there is a connection between the gender of an elderly person and the carer. Mothers prefer to be looked after by daughters, for instance – and fathers, by sons. Since the majority of elderly people requiring help are women, then a great deal of the responsibliity for looking after them will fall on women's shoulders.

Discrimination against carers

We have a long way to go before society really shifts in attitude, and both men and women assume that caring is not only a woman's job. Meanwhile, we have a situation where women find themselves discriminated against and often in a disadvantaged position because they are caring for others.

Not only are men more likely to recieve increased back-up support from professional services such as health visitors, home helps and nurses, they are also likely to receive more informal help from relatives, friends and neighbours. Men are somehow seen as more in need. Until recently, even though a man who had to give up his job to care for someone at home was eligible for invalid care allowance, a co-habitating or married woman who did the same, was not eligible. However, following the campaign of certain organisations and individuals like Jaqueline Drake, things are looking up.

Jaqueline had retired from her job early to care for her 69-year-old mother with senile dementia, and was outraged to find that because she had a husband she did not qualify for the invalid care allowance. Eventually, after appealing her case for years in the UK, she took it to the European Court which agreed that there must be equal opportunities to claim social security benefits, and that discrimination on the grounds of either sex or marital status must end. So Jaqueline and other women like her should now receive the invalid care allowance.

The Family Policy Studies Centre (address on page 146) calls women carers 'the forgotten army' and says they provide a service which saves the government billions of pounds a year. It is only justice that the laws should be altered in their favour. Caring is a costly business, and even though there are other benefits available, such as attendance allowance for the person being cared for, and also grants to help with alterations and improvements, a great deal of extra expense is paid for by the carers themselves — for example, special diets and extra heating.

Furthermore, over retiring age the invalid care allowance ends for both men and women because this particular benefit is supposedly based on the carer's loss of income after having to give up work. In view of the extra expense involved in caring, which is usually even more difficult for someone to afford on a pension, these discrepancies urgently need sorting out.

The physical toll of caring

It is good to know that there is now a growing number of organisations working on behalf of carers to bring their problems to the attention of the public and the government. For instance, the Association of Carers (address on page 145) was founded in 1981 by Judith Oliver who knows from experience what it is like to look after a disabled husband for many years. The association is in touch with thousands of people caring for relatives and friends and has learned a great deal about the difficulties they face.

The problems are not just financial, but emotional, social and physical. Carers can be completely tied to their homes, their days a daily round of housework, laundry, dressing, feeding and toiletting which consumes a great deal of time and effort. Especially among older women, as Judith Oliver discovered, this will also take its toll on their own physical and mental well-being. The most common complaints are those of back pain, exacerbation of arthritis and gynaecological problems such as prolapse.

It is interesting to note that in a guidance booklet produced by the Royal College of Nursing, the assumption throughout is that two people will be lifting a person out of a chair or bed. This is seldom the case with home nursing. In addition, there are the complications of their own ill-health which many carers have to try to ignore:

《 *Having reached a situation where healthcare in the form of surgery, physiotherpy or whatever is needed, they are unable to take advantage of the treatment available. Many say they have had to turn down surgery, for instance, because they could not find alternative care for their dependants when a bed became available.*

'Others say they were unable to comply with the surgeons instructions that they undertake no lifting or pulling for a period of time after the operation. Yet others say that the dependant refused to allow them to go away and would not receive help from another source while the carer was receiving treatment. For example, one member of the Association of Carers had to leave hospital within two days of a mastectomy with her draining tubes still in place because the community nursing service found her mother and disabled husband too much to cope with. 》

Increasingly, situations like the ones cited affect the mental health of carers. Many live in fear of what the future will bring and also whether their own health will hold. Yet if they report to a GP or social worker with complaints about this, they risk being written off as neurotic middle-aged women.

The Association of Carers is campaigning vigorously on their behalf for more professional and financial support. It also provides a counselling service and a range of literature with advice on emotional as well as practical problems. Their booklet *Help at Hand* is particularly useful. Another helping organisation, the Family Welfare Association (address on page 146) has produced *Keeping Fit While Caring* which contains a step-by-step guide to lifting without injury and other hints.

Support from other carers

There are other groups starting up for carers, some backed by local Age Concerns and other voluntary organisations such as the National Council for Carers and their Elderly Dependents. Other groups run by local authority health or social services departments may be in conjunction with a day centre, where elderly and disabled people can spend one, two, or even more, days a week.

Self-help groups have also been started by carers themselves, many of which form a strong platform to campaign for improvements in health facilities, patients' rights and benefits, public awareness and funds for research. A useful leaflet giving advice on organising such a group is issued by Age Well, a project run by Age Concern and the Health Education Council to promote better health for older people. As their leaflet explains, the most important fact in self-help is togetherness. A problem shared is usually a problem halved, whether it is learning how to cope with rheumatism, wanting to lose some weight or caring for an elderly relative.

However, many carers may not have a great deal of energy left over for campaigning, and may simply want to go along to the group for support, advice and a break from usual responsibilities. At first, one social worker organising such a group invited speakers to talk about different aspects of caring and disability. But after a year, and at the request of members, there were discussions held on all sorts of other subjects. The evening turned into a much needed social outing.

For some, in fact, this meeting may be the only evening out they have during the month; and it is often the encouragement and moral support they get from the group that gives them the resolve to come at all. Many carers, due to a mixture of their own unnecessary guilt and the emotional blackmail exerted by dependents, can be easily manipulated and feel bad about leaving them. As a woman who looks after both her mother and husband explained:

« *Mother makes me feel guilty. If I stand up to her, she looks so sad and that makes me feel wicked. But in a way she dominates me more now than when I was young. I only come out once a month, but she tries to stop me. Coming here they say things like 'You must think of yourself, you have to say enough's enough.' That helps me a lot and I find I'm able to assert myself a bit more. I had a meal out with a friend recently, and now we've got mother into hospital for a few weeks so that I can take my husband away on holiday.* »

Someone looking after a partner or relative with Alzheimer's disease – or senile dementia as it is also known – has particular problems. Although the person suffering from the disorder may be physically fit, the deterioration of the brain's function leads to very distressing and anti-social behaviour at times.

The Alzheimer's Disease Society (address on page 145) offers counselling and useful literature to help with coping. Local groups also hold meetings with speakers at which those caring for relatives or friends with the condition can learn more. The local Oxford group, for instance, has a meeting every six weeks with talks on medical treatments, new research findings and practical and financial aids available for home care. Just as important is the talk over a cup of tea at the end when members share common problems. This group also has a sitting-in service, which is often necessary for carers if they are going to be able to get away and attend meetings at all.

The Chest, Heart and Stroke Association (address on page 145) has counsellors who can give advice both to the patients and to the person caring for them. Particularly in the case of a heart attack or stroke, a whole family's way of life can be drastically altered overnight; and there is often a need for emotional support as much as practical advice.

The emotional support of an outside group can be very helpful in sorting out a carer's feelings of guilt and anger, which are very common reactions. Particularly in the case of partners, the one doing the caring may sometimes feel considerable resentment at the changes in the relationship and the demands made, and then suffer guilt because of this. By talking through such emotions with a trained counsellor, people are helped to come to terms with their more negative feelings and accept that these are normal and common to a stressful situation.

Support and self-help groups are also getting started for people from ethnic minorities who often find themselves more isolated than anyone else when ill or when caring for someone who is dependent. One such group for Greek Cypriot women meets for a lunch club where they cook traditional dishes and work on embroidery together. The meeting also provides a good opportunity to learn about the sort of medical and financial assistance available – useful for anyone who speaks little English.

In London the needs of people from ethnic groups are being looked into by other organisations like the Standing Conference of Ethnic Minority Senior Citizens (address on page 155). There is evidence, for instance, that the idea of the supportive extended family is often a myth, and one Birmingham survey showed that among Asian people over a quarter had no close relatives in Britain. Often it is on caring friends and neighbours that the responsibility of looking after such people falls.

Support from statutory services

Professional services available to the carer come from various sources and vary a great deal from area to area. So, depending on where you live, there may be quite a lot of help to call upon, or there may be very little. Enquiries at local hospitals, your local Age Concern group, the community health council and social services should give the broad outline of what exists.

The most common services supplied by social services are home helps, laundry service, meals on wheels and day care centres. Community nurses and health visitors are available through the NHS. Nurses visit someone at home once or twice a week, helping with bathing, dressing, lifting and medical care, and providing incontinence pads. Sometimes visits will be on a regular daily basis, especially when a person is very disabled and assistance is needed in getting up and putting to bed.

Even so, the total care of someone who is dependent can be very draining, especially when you are growing older yourself, and what is needed as well is the chance of a break from the routine.

Day care schemes run by voluntary organisations and social services departments, to which older people can go for a few hours daily, are very helpful. As well as a mid-day meal, stimulating activities are arranged; and these, plus the company, can make an enjoyable break for the cared for as well as the carer. However, there can be some resistance to start with. A partner may hate feeling dependent, but still find it difficult to get out of the house and mix with strangers. None of us likes upheavals, and if you're elderly you may like them even less than other people. Suggestions from a member of the family may be particularly unwelcome. A third party, perhaps a social worker, might be more suitable.

Anne who took full responsibility for the care of her husband, David, who had suffered a stroke, needed a rest for a couple of days a week as she was suffering from arthritis. David was so upset about the prospect of going to a day centre that when the ambulance arrived he had uncharacteristic temper tantrums on the doorstep. To pacify him and avoid the embarrassment of neighbours hearing, Anne gave in.

Eventually, on the advice of other members of the family, their GP was called to talk to David. He explained that Anne needed support too and that if he wanted to stay at home most of the time, then he must consider her welfare and go to the centre sometimes as well. David agreed to go and ended up liking it.

Neighbourhood and care attendant schemes

Another kind of support are the various care attendant schemes coming into operation. Many of these are arranged through a voluntary organisation called Crossroads (address on page 143) which takes its name from the television series because of the attention it focussed on the needs of disabled people. The first Crossroads Care Attendant Scheme, paying trained helpers to go into the home, started in Rugby, and there are now about sixty schemes in operation throughout the country, with more to come. Each works independently with its own management committee under the umbrella of Crossroads, adapting to the special needs and services of a particular area.

Some social services departments have started neighbourhood care schemes, paying suitable people to go into someone's home and help care for a disabled person. Other care attendant services have been started by self-help organisations. The Redbridge Care Attendant Scheme, for instance, was set up by a local association for handicapped people with funding from various sources, including the Greater London Association for the Disabled (address on page 146). The care attendants are carefully chosen and trained, and are able to help a large cross section of people tied to their homes looking after someone else.

Joan's husband suffers from motor neurone disease, is very weak and has been in a wheelchair for the last nine years, almost totally dependent on her for physical care. She gets some help from their son who lives with them and works night shifts and from a care attendant once a week for a three-hour session who makes lunch and supervises James' toilet care. His presence gives Joan some respite and complements the assistance she receives from the doctor who visits once a week and a nurse who comes in the morning and at night to put James to bed.

For a longer break for carers such as holidays, a new idea growing in popularity is a family placement scheme for elderly people which works in a similar way to short-term fostering for children and teenagers. An Age Concern report featuring three such schemes in Liverpool, Leicestershire and Leeds found they were proving very successful, often leading to a general improvement in the relationship between carer and cared for.

Many of the people fostering older people are middle-aged women themselves whose children have left home and whose parents or partner has died. They are often already experienced in the needs of those they are looking after, and a close relationship can build up between them and the whole family.

Facing up to the alternatives

If, in the end, the situation becomes too difficult and the burden of caring too great, then you as the carer shouldn't feel guilty about considering nursing or residential care, either short or long-term.

When faced with the decision about choosing a residential or rest home, you will need to discuss admission to a local authority home with a social worker. If you want to investigate one run by a voluntary or private organisation, be aware that these establishments vary considerably in the standards of facilities provided.

Details of provision can be obtained from social services and from organisations such as Counsel and Care for the Elderly and GRACE. Private nursing homes are registered with the district health authority, and the Registered Nursing Homes Association will have details about the facilities (addresses on pages 155-6).

Of course in addition to the feelings of the person being cared for and the carer, there is also the expense of private nursing and residential care. At the time of writing, part of the cost can be met by state benefits. Some people who need extra care and can afford the cost actually choose it, perhaps because they understand the advantages of releasing a daughter and other family members from the 24-hour responsibility of caring.

Betty's mother is suffering from a mild form of senile dementia, and the family has decided residential care will be best for her. She talks all the time and craves company – something her family were simply unable to provide at home. As Betty explained: 'We'll still be visiting a lot, particularly once I've stopped working, but in the home she will have the company and the care that quite honestly is beyond us now. I think it will be better for all of us, mother included. In fact she is looking forward to it.'

The sad fact is that the greater the need, the less outside help is usually available. Though it may be possible to get professional or voluntary back-up for a few hours a day or a few days a week, an old or very sick and disabled person needs constant nursing and supervision round the clock. In these circumstances, the back-up resources are not there, and care for the carers is also needed.

If the demands of caring are not beyond them and the statutory and community support is available, other carers 'stay the course'. They are rewarded with the deep satisfaction of having seen a loved one through what is often the hardest period of their lives, with all its opportunities for expressing affection and support.

Further reading

Care Attendant Schemes
GLAD, 1986*

Carers and Services, Caring for the Elderly and Handicapped, Who Cares for the Carers?
Equal Opportunities Commission*

Caring: Experiences of Looking After Disabled Relatives
Anna Briggs and Judith Oliver, Routledge and Kegan Paul, 1985

Caring For An Elderly Relative
Keith Thompson, Martin Dunitz, 1986

Elderly People: Rights and Opportunities
Jill Manthorpe, Longman, 1986

Help at Hand
Association of Carers*

Keeping Fit While Caring
Family Welfare Association, 1984*

Take Care of Your Elderly Relative
Dr J A Muir Gray and H McKenzie, Penguin, 1986

The 36-Hour Day
Mace, Robins, Castleton, Cloke, McEwen, Age Concern England, 1986

Agewell Ideas Pack
Age Concern England, 1986. Free

Attendance Allowance NI 205
Invalid Care Allowance NI 212
Looking After Someone at Home (Home Responsibilities Protection) NI 27
Invalidity Benefit NI 16A
Going into Hospital NI 9
Non-contributory Invalidity Pension NI 210
Department of Health and Social Security

*Address on pages 145-6.

Taking care of yourself
Vivien Donald's guidelines for keeping healthy

*T*oday we are bombarded with advice on what to eat, what to avoid. We are told to exercise, but then again told that too much exercise can be a bad thing for those of a certain age. It is all very confusing and tedious, especially as most of the advice is either geared to middle-aged men, women with growing families or the young and active.

We know that it pays to be informed about the particular problems of getting older, like osteoporosis, the development of brittle bones, that can afflict women past the menopause. And we also know that maintaining good health is a matter of having the right routine, getting into good habits. Retirement is an ideal time to take stock and consider which habits are worth acquiring, now that there is plenty of time for regular exercise and for preparing nutritious food.

What kind of exercise?

The important thing about exercise is to know what kind is safe and how much is enough. Regular exercising not only keeps the body supple; it strengthens heart and lungs and helps increase relaxation and reduces stress. If you find yourself panting after climbing the stairs, or stiff after unaccustomed physical work, such as gardening, it's nature's way of telling you that you could benefit from extra exercise. But plunging enthusiastically into a too strenuous programme is often an extremely painful answer that may result in a period of enforced rest!

It is best to start slowly and unambitiously at first. Walking to the shops instead of taking the car or bus, or walking up the stairs instead of using the lift are comparatively painless ways of working towards greater things. Within two or three weeks a brisk walk for a full half-hour becomes an enjoyable experience. You may feel ready to embark on more strenuous exercise; but do talk to your doctor before you get carried away if you have a history of heart trouble or high blood pressure, or any other health problems such as bronchitis or emphysema.

The best approach is to do a little hard work every day, exercising enough to become breathless and increase the heart beat. Leg and arm muscles should be exercised just a little bit longer after they feel tired, and tendons and muscles should be well stretched.

Combining the three S's

There are three main aims of exercise programmes: to increase stamina (for heart and lungs); strength (for muscles) and suppleness (to benefit muscles, ligaments and tendons). Some activities are good for one or two of the three S's and not for others, but different ones can be combined to give the best overall results. The activities listed below are starred according to their fitness rating and their effect on the body.

Exercise	Strength	Stamina	Suppleness
Cycling	* * * *legs*	* * *	* *
Dancing	* * *	* * *	* *
Gardening, housework	* *	* *	*
Keep fit, music and movement	* * *	* * *	* * *
Swimming	* * *	* * *	* *
Walking	* * *legs*	* *	*
Yoga	* * *	* * *	* * *

Although exercise will be working properly only if it is vigorous enough to cause some sweating and panting, you can check what it is doing to your heart, if you fear overstraining, by monitoring the pulse rate. The safe rate per minute is calculated according to age: that is, your age subtracted from 170. For a woman of 60, for instance, it works like this: $170 - 60 = 110$.

As you begin to get breathless after starting exercise, stop and take the pulse rate (count the beats for 30 seconds and then multiply by two to give the rate per minute). If the rate goes higher than your 'safe' calculation, stop frequently to rest during exercise until you are fitter. The ideal to aim for is 15 to 20 minutes at the calculated rate every day to maintain heart and lung stamina, and once fitness is achieved, three sessions a week are enough. If at any time any exercise causes severe discomfort, pain or extreme breathlessness, stop doing it and see your doctor.

Despite those veterans seen in the marathons, jogging is tough on the joints and better left to the young and the truly athletic. A brisk walk, combined with exercise for suppleness, is more suitable. Jazz and dance exercise and aerobics are likely to be too demanding at the pace established in many classes. Square and country dancing are fun and good exercise, too; now that tea dancing is back in fashion, there's the chance to get into ballroom dancing as well. Age Concern runs tea dances, as do some local authorities, hotels and dance halls.

For aching joints you can't beat swimming as an exercise. The support of the water makes light of stiffness and lack of agility. Some pools run special swimming groups for older people (who may prefer to swim when there are no youngsters around), and adult classes for those who have never learnt to swim. Arthritis sufferers will also find cycling is good for the joints.

Adult education centres also hold day and evening keep-fit classes for older people, and the Women's League of Health and Beauty have classes tailored to meet different abilities (address on page 151). Yoga and Tai Chi, the Chinese system of daily exercise and martial art, are excellent for relieving stress. A period of mental relaxation is one of the ingredients of a typical Yoga class, and there are also classes devoted entirely to meditation. Local libraries have information about classes held in the area.

There are many other activities and sports that are just as suitable for older women as they are for younger ones: golf, badminton, skiing (cross country or downhill), croquet, table tennis, bowling, rambling, sailing, archery – anything that is, and continues to be, enjoyable. The pace may be different, but the fun remains the same.

Exercising at home

If you decide to exercise at home (and there are many programmes and routines on tape, in magazines and in books) remember to start slowly and build up gradually, following the warming-up exercise faithfully at the beginning and end of the programme. Few exercise routines are designed for the 55-plus age range, so don't do anything that hurts or is exhausting. It's more fun and is likely to be done more regularly if you share your exercise sessions with a neighbour or friend. Anyone who has difficulty in getting down to the floor and up is safer exercising on a firm mattress.

If you cannot get out and about, you can continue to be active, either doing housework or gardening (there are aids to help disabled gardeners) or doing exercises suggested by the health visitor, district nurse or doctor. Simply tightening muscles, and putting all the joints through a full range of movements, from toes to neck, will help anyone who is chairbound.

Healthy eating and drinking

Some of the problems associated with old age can be warded off by eating enough of the right foods. Since overweight (or obesity, to use a less flattering word) is linked with many health problems, eating less of the wrong foods is essential, too. Making sure of a balanced diet means, essentially, eating a selection of different foods, with no one type predominating. It's mainly a question of the basic commonsense stuff we all know. Natural foods such as fruit, raw or lightly-cooked vegetables and wholemeal bread are good for vitamins and fibre and help to prevent constipation. Animal fats and refined sugar contribute to a weight problem and can be a factor in heart and arterial disease. Sugar, of course, can lead to tooth decay (so that some foods, such as meat, become difficult to eat) and also to diabetes.

Too much salt is also to be avoided, as it is implicated in high blood pressure, heart disease and fluid retention. We lose some of the sense of taste as we get older, but the temptation to add more salt to food, and to eat salty foods, should be resisted – salt is best added only at the cooking stage; not at the table. Get the habit of flavouring with mild spices, herbs and other natural seasonings.

Only very few older people are likely to suffer protein or vitamin deficiency, and when this does occur the deficiency is usually caused either by a specific type of disease or by the diet not being properly balanced. But a small deficiency can occur through struggling to manage on a low income, through a difficulty in swallowing or chewing food, not bothering to plan a nourishing diet, or difficulty in shopping because of a disability. And some doctors think that as we get older our bodies are less efficient in taking up some nutrients in food, so extra amounts may be needed. Vitamin C is an example, also some minerals such as calcium.

If your diet is based on a cultural background originating from a hotter country, you may be lacking in vitamin D, which is absorbed through sunlight, as well as being present in food. Darker skin colour is nature's protection against the sun's harmful rays, but it can be a disadvantage in a sunless climate. This can result in anaemia and osteomalacia (a type of old-age rickets). People from Asian communities, particularly, need to be sure they are having enough vitamin D.

Nutritional value of foods

The following list of the main nutrients in food shows that if there is one type of food that you don't like, or find too expensive, it is possible to substitute another within the same group to keep the diet balanced.

- Proteins (the essential building blocks of the body's cells): in meat, liver, fish, dairy products, bread and flour, peas, beans, lentils and nuts.

- Carbohydrates (starches and sugars): bread and flour, rice and other cereals, pasta, potatotes and other root vegetables. Less good for you are sugary drinks, sweets and jams.

- Fat: lard and cooking fat, oils, margarine, butter, suet, fats in meat and fish, dairy products, fried foods, pastries and cakes. Fats should be used sparingly by everyone and avoided as much as possible by those who are overweight or have heart disease or high blood pressure.

- Vitamin A (for healthy eyes): margarine and dairy products (except cheeses made from skimmed milk), liver, kidney, cod liver oil, leafy and salad vegetables, some fruits (apricots, peaches, cantaloupe and watermelon).

- Vitamin B group (for energy, nerves and skin): meat, bacon, liver and kidney, bread and flour, yeast, milk and dairy products, vegetables including potatoes, fish roes. Some foods, such as breakfast cereals, are also fortified with B group vitamins.

- Vitamin C (for gums and faster healing; may help prevent atherosclerosis, thickening of the arteries): fruits, (especially citrus, blackcurrants and berries), green leafy vegetables and potatoes. Anyone worried that citrus fruits are too acid will be relieved to learn that they become alkaline during digestion.

- Vitamin D (important in helping the assimilation of calcium, as a protection against osteoporosis, and for teeth): oily fish (herrings, kippers, mackerel, sardines), margarine, butter, eggs, fish roe and liver.

- Calcium (for bones and teeth, particularly important for women after the menopause as a prevention against osteoporosis): milk, yoghurt, cheeses, cream, calcium fortified bread (that is, all breads except 100 per cent wholemeal), canned or soused fish with bones, green leafy vegetables (watercress, kale, spring greens, etc).

- Iron (for blood): liver, kidney, meat, bacon, egg yolk, bread and flour, green leafy vegetables, dried fruit, cocoa, oily fish (sardines, sprats, pilchards).

- Dietary fibre (roughage): bread and flour, especially wholemeal, cereals, especially bran and wholegrains. Other foods that contain fibre – but are not as fibre-rich – are vegetables, pulses, fruit (eaten with the skin), nuts and dried fruits.

The average recommended daily allowances (RDAs) that are accepted as being necessary for a healthy and balanced diet for a woman in the UK are as follows:

Energy   **2,000 cals**
Protein   **50g**
Fats   **77g**
Carbohydrate   **275g**
Fibre   **25-30g**

The RDAs for vitamins and minerals vary between different countries, with America and Russia often recommending a higher daily amounts than the UK. The UK recommendation for vitamin C is 30mg, while in the USA it is 60mg; and if you drink or smoke, your need for vitamin C is increased, as explained on page 107. Also energy requirements vary with body size and how active you are, so the figures quoted above should be taken as a rough guide.

For calcium, the RDA in the UK is 500mg, while the American recommendation is 800mg. However, post-menopausal women need 1,000-1,500mg daily to help avoid osteoporosis, as explained further on page 113.

Overcooking destroys vitamins, so vegetables are best eaten either raw or lightly cooked, and as some vitamins are lost after harvesting, the sooner the vegetables are eaten, the better – a good argument for having a small vegetable plot. Keeping vegetables in the fridge, and preparing them just before they are to be cooked, helps preserve the vitamin content, too. This vitamin loss is a reason why those expensive ready-made and overcooked convenience foods are not as nourishing.

It's only in the last few years that everyone has begun talking seriously about fibre in diet, although those who have always eaten a breakfast that includes all-bran have known for years about the virtues of fibre. Cereal fibre, which includes the bran in wholemeal flour, wholemeal bread and bran itself, acts as a very effective way of preventing constipation, diverticular disease and other bowel complaints. Diverticular disease is a condition of the bowel caused by abnormal activity of the bowel wall when your diet contains insufficient fibre. This complaint is said to affect one person in three over the age of 60 in the West.

The amount of fibre needed each day – 25 to 30mg – may already be a part of your diet. If you eat brown rice, wholegrain cereals such as Weetabix, porridge or muesli, pulses (particularly baked beans or processed peas) or two slices of wholemeal bread, you may be having enough to prevent constipation. If more is needed, try a breakfast cereal that contains bran, or sprinkle bran over another cereal. Experiment with just a teaspoonful at first, increasing up to $1\frac{1}{2}$/2oz (15g) gradually, as necessary. Too much bran introduced all at once to a stomach that is unused to it could cause discomfort and wind! Don't overdo the bran in any case – too much can affect the absorption of calcium.

Here is a suggested daily diet

- Two slices of whole meal bread or a portion of breakfast cereal with natural bran
- One orange or other fresh fruit
- Half a pint of milk
- One portion of eggs, cheese, fish, meat or poultry. Meat should not be eaten more than once a day; and fish is increasingly thought of as healthier – oily fish is useful in the prevention of

heart disease and arthritis – and you may feel it is worth substituting fish for meat as a main meal twice a week.

Supplementing your diet

As a supplement to a normal diet, there are multi-vitamins and vitamin-plus mineral tablets that can be bought over the counter at pharmacists and health food stores. These may be helpful when recovering from an illness or if you fear your normal diet is lacking. You can ask the pharmacist for advice about the one that would be best for you. Many people take vitamin C supplements at the beginning of a cold or flu, but excessive amounts can cause kidney stones, diarrhoea and dyspepsia. However, if you're eating a healthy diet, you don't need supplements; and if you think you need a supplement like calcium, this should be prescribed and supervised by a doctor.

There are some illnesses and drugs that can cause vitamin deficiencies, and your doctor should advise on supplements. Conditions that can result in a need for supplements include peptic ulcer, hiatus hernia and diverticular disease which can lead to iron-deficiency anaemia. Diarrhoea, kidney disease and taking a diuretic drug may lead to potassium deficiency which can result in depression, weak muscles and mental confusion. Potassium-rich foods include bananas, milky coffee, orange juice, raisins and sultanas.

Diuretic drugs can also cause thiamine deficiency which can be helped by taking extra vitamin B1 found in brewer's yeast and wheatgerm. There are a few people who develop sores or cracked skin at the corner of the mouth and suffer from riboflavin or vitamin B2 deficiency. Riboflavin is present in whole grains, eggs, green leafy vegetables, peas and liver.

Scurvy, the old sailor's disease, is caused by a lack of vitamin C. Tobacco, generous amounts of alcohol and aspirin interfere with vitamin C absorption; the Americans recommend a 60mg daily supplement for smokers or drinkers and this may be a reasonable amount to try.

If you feel that you are lacking in energy, and are feeling tired and listless, it may be that you are suffering from anaemia, which can be remedied by iron tablets (your doctor can give you a simple blood test to check for anaemia).

The cost of providing good food may seem frighteningly high. One way of cutting costs of course is to get together with other people and bulk buy items such as rice, pulses, flour and cereals. If you have to have a special diet for health reasons, and find you cannot afford the price, make sure you are claiming the supplementary benefits to which you are entitled. If you have a disability that makes cooking a problem, ask your health visitor for advice about aids and adaptations for the kitchen.

There are plenty of good recipes suitable for health-conscious people in the many 'healthy living' magazines on newstands, not to mention newspaper articles and the books listed on pages 121-2.

How much should you drink?

Plenty of fluid during the day – as much as 3 to 5 pints – is recommended, in the form of tea, coffee, water and fruit juices, or other non-alcoholic beverages. Alcohol in moderation is all right, too. Have a sherry before your meal or a glass of wine with it, or a glass of spirits – it's only drinking to excess that leads to problems, including loss of appetite and liver damage.

Remember that tolerance to alcohol decreases with age. The equivalent of 2 pints of beer, 2 doubles of spirits or 4 glasses of wine is probably the maximum that can be safely drunk regularly – and women's bodies tolerate less than men's. If you are in the habit of drinking more than you think you should, try having two alcohol-free days every week. While 4 glasses of wine is considered safe, more than that could be taking you into the danger area of getting cirrhosis of the liver. There are also the dangers of cutting down on food to pay for drink or drifting into excessive drinking due to loneliness.

Keeping your weight down

Overweight is caused by eating more energy-giving foods than are needed, so that the excess is turned into fat instead of being burned up. Some people unfortunately gain more weight on less food than others who remain slim (unfairly) even while they eat cakes and pastries.

Losing weight is more difficult as we get older, and it is infuriatingly easy for the weight to shoot back up again if dieting is relaxed. Combining a slimming diet with exercise, even that brisk extra thirty minutes' walk every day, will gradually show satisfying results.

There are many calorie counting booklets and slimming books available, but most experts agree that the best type of dieting is a change to new eating habits, based on the type of balanced diet outlined earlier in the chapter, and on eating less of the high energy foods – fats and refined carbohydrates (sugars). Bread and potatoes, although they are carbohydrate foods, are known as unrefined carbohydrates and are not especially rich in energy, so you can eat them – but with mininum butter or margarine. They also contain fibre.

Fried and fatty meats are best avoided, but fat can be cut off before cooking, and meat or fish can be grilled or cooked in the oven. Cottage or other low-fat cheese can be substituted for full-fat cheese; skimmed and semi-skimmed milk for whole milk. Look for low-fat products; although butter and margarine normally have the same number of calories (210 per 1oz/28g), there are low-fat spreads with only half as many. Fats should contribute less than a third of the total energy in your diet.

Dieting also means keeping a close eye on the prepared foods that you buy and cutting them out if they include energy-rich ingredients. Examples include mayonnaise, pastry and fried snacks, crisps, fruit-flavoured yogurts and canned soft drinks. For calorie counters, 1,500 to 2,000 calories per day should be enough to maintain correct weight and carry on an active life. If you need to lose a large amount of weight, you should talk over with your doctor the possibility of a very low calorie diet, such as the Cambridge Diet. Though only about 600 calories are allowed daily, the diet is considered appropriate by doctors where there is real health risk, as in the case of high blood pressure, for instance.

Very low-calorie diets need to be undertaken with some kind of supervision, and are usually best suited to anyone with more than two stones to lose. Any sudden or unexplained change in weight, either loss or a gain, should be reported to a doctor.

Looking after your health

The menopause and after

Average age for the ceasing of menstruation is around 50, but the hot flushes and sweating that can accompany it are more common after the periods have ended, and may last from just a few months to more than five years. About a quarter of women have no symptoms at all, but in a further quarter they are more severe and long-lasting, and result from hormonal changes in the body. These changes also cause loss of lubrication and thinning of the walls of the vagina, and lead to osteoporosis (brittle bones) in later life. All may be helped by hormone replacement therapy (HRT) or by alternative self-help methods.

Hot flushes are caused by the capillaries suddenly filling with blood to give a sudden rush to the face, neck and shoulders, with extra body heat and perspiration. They may happen once or twice a week or several times in an hour. If hot flushes persist or cause discomfort and disturb sleep well after the menopause, ask your doctor if HRT would be helpful (details below). There are self-help ways to lessen discomfort, too, such as taking vitamin B6 (pyridoxine). Ginseng is another alternative, but it is expensive and should not be taken for more than a month, as doctors suspect it is harmful to those who have high blood pressure. For more details of self-help, see Further reading at the end of the chapter.

The fall in oestrogen levels during the menopause affects the layers of cells in the vagina so that they become thinner, with less lubrication and elasticity and intercourse can become painful, making the vagina sore (a condition called dyspareunia). This does not happen to all women, who may continue to lubricate effectively during sexual stimulation. Dryness and thinning can leave the vagina vulnerable to infection, so anyone with a history of cystitis, itching or pruritis needs to take extra care with hygiene; but avoid over-enthusiastic washing. HRT can help with vaginal dryness, or a doctor can prescribe a hormonal (oestrogen) cream to be inserted in the vagina. There are lubricants like KY jelly and Senselle to buy from chemists without prescription – and considerably more pleasant to use than petroleum jelly.

Exercise that can help to maintain the elasticity of the vagina are also used to control urinary incontinence and avoid a prolapse –

they are the pelvic floor exercises that women are taught to do after childbirth: sit on the lavatory with the thighs parallel to the ground and feet flat on the floor (or on a book, if necessary); start to pass water, then use the muscles to stop the flow; release and finish the flow. This may sound somewhat awesome but it is fairly easy to accomplish. Within a few days you will have identified the relevant muscles needed to stop the flow. The exercise can be done regularly without flow at any time that you are sitting – in the car, in the office – or while standing. Build up slowly to a frequency of 20 muscle-pulls six to eight times a day.

Hormone replacement therapy consists of the hormones oestrogen and progesterone taken daily to help replace those lost or produced erratically at the menopause. This treatment can reduce hot flushes and vaginal thinning and is also highly effective against osteoporosis. It is reckoned to be capable of cutting the death rate from fractures in older women by 60 per cent and may also protect against heart disease and rheumatoid arthritis.

Little is known about how and why these last two conditions are helped, but it is known that protection against osteoporosis lasts only as long as the treatment is taken. Some women in America are prepared to continue with hormone replacement for life.

Few doctors would recommend such long-term use. There are thought to be risks of developing cancer of the breast or lining of the womb as a result of HRT, and it is not recommended if there is a family history of heart disease, breast or womb cancer, or if you have high blood pressure, blood clotting problems, a heart disorder or gall bladder disease. If you are on HRT, thorough checkups are needed on a regular basis, and long-term treatment, if it is maintained, will require checks at six-monthly intervals.

If you feel you could benefit from HRT, but your doctor refuses even to consider it, you can visit a private or NHS menopause clinic at a hospital independently for a consultation there. Look in the telephone directory for the number of your local health authority, who can give you the address of your nearest menopausal clinic and ask, when you speak to the clinic, whether they will accept you without a doctor's referral.

Coping with cystitis

This problem, an inflammation of the lining of the bladder, has been described as the desire to rush to the loo every five minutes in order to produce two burning drops! There are several self-help ways of coping with it. Most importantly, drink plenty of fluids (but not coffee or alcohol). One teaspoonful of bicarbonate of soda in a glass of water three times a day, or potassium citrate (sachets can be bought from the pharmacist) help to make the urine less acid. Do answer the call of nature, even if there are only two burning drops, so that the acid contents of the bladder is emptied. If your stomach feels tender and you have a slight temperature (cystitis is an infection) the best remedy is to go to bed with a hot water bottle wrapped in a towel against your stomach.

If the cystitis is still troubling you after one or two days, see your doctor, who will be able to give you an antibiotic. Apart from special care with hygiene (use non-medicated and unperfumed soap and avoid toiletries such as bath oils and bubble baths) you can do a lot to prevent cystitis by wearing cotton pants and loose rather than tight-fitting trousers. It is worth remembering that with increasing age, the symptoms of cystitis may be less dramatic but it can cause incontinence of urine. See also Further reading at the end of the chapter.

Osteoporosis and back pain

Brittle bones is a condition that affects all older people to some degree, but post-menopausal women in particular; and it is the reason why they break their bones so easily if they fall. As many as 40 per cent of women over 65 suffer fractures that are caused by osteoporosis. It is caused by a loss of calcium in the bones that makes them become softer, porous and weaker.

Risk of developing osteoporosis is greatest once past the menopause, but there is also a risk in anyone who has had an early menopause after removal of the ovaries; in those who are underweight, and who are white with 'transparent' skin (black women suffer fewer fractures). A history of osteoporosis in the family is a factor; as are diseases such as diabetes, gastro-intestinal disorders, inflammatory arthritis, kidney and liver disease. Drugs such as anticoagulants, antacids, barbiturates, alcohol and tobacco may increase the likelihood of the condition developing. Some medical treatments, such as partial gastrectomy, may also lead to osteoporosis.

Diet and exercise are the major ways to prevent osteoporosis. Cutting down on smoking and alcohol are sensible moves. Increasing calcium in the diet as recommended earlier in this chapter is another, along with vitamin D – both needed to aid bone metabolism.

One of the best ways of getting enough vitamin D is to go out into the sunshine. Fifteen minutes of sunshine in the middle of the day (11am to 4pm), even beside an open window if you can't get outside, between April and October will provide plenty of vitamin D. Diet can be boosted in winter with one helping each week of foods rich in vitamin D: herring, kippers, mackerel or sardines (see also pages 104-5).

Regular exercise helps to strengthen and thicken bones, especially the amounts and types of exercise discussed at the beginning of this chapter; and for those less agile, there are exercises recommended for the prevention of osteoporosis. Toe touches and sit-ups should be avoided; they are particularly harmful to anyone who has osteoporosis in the spine. Slouching is also bad for you – good posture, whether you are sitting or standing, will protect your spine against becoming curved.

If your back gives you trouble, you may already have decided that finding a cure is as elusive as the Holy Grail, and that learning how to prevent back pain, and cope with it when it is unavoidable is the best way of living with it. An important part of the preventive routine is keeping up good posture, whether standing, sitting or walking. It can be a real effort to avoid slumping, but the relief of a straight-backed chair that supports the lower back, a pillow in the lap to support sewing or knitting or a lectern for reading is immeasurable. Lifting even a small object wrongly can do damage, too; lifting should always be done with a straight back, bending at the knees and using thigh muscles.

Organise the work surfaces in your kitchen to the right height (at wrist level when you are standing beside it) and avoid slouching with all your weight on one leg when washing up or ironing. Loads should be divided equally before carrying them, so that there is no one-sided strain – and remember not to twist your back as you dump shopping on to a car seat. Sleep on a firm mattress – or, better still, a plank under the mattress.

It may be that osteopathy or chiropractic could help; and both osteopaths and chiropractors have had a long training which includes medical education and qualifies them to give valuable help with backache. Although some doctors carry on the tradition of the medical profession in refusing to accept these 'outsiders', more are now realising that osteopaths and chiropractors can relieve pain. So if you ask your doctor about extra help, don't accept a negative response, unless he/she is able to explain why these alternative methods would not help you.

Your doctor may be able to recommend an osteopath or chiropractor, or you may be able to find one through a friend or in the *Yellow Pages*. Check with the relevant professional organisation that the one you choose is registered, and is therefore properly qualified. Unfortunately this kind of therapy is not available free within the NHS.

Heart disease and high blood pressure

Younger women are protected from heart disease, but once past the menopause we become as vulnerable as men, especially if we don't exercise, are overweight and smoke. Most doctors agree that diet plays a part in prevention of heart disease – less animal fats and more fibre are thought best – as discussed earlier. But it is not altogether clear what part dietary habits play. Polyunsaturated fats may reduce the amount of fatty deposits in the arteries which cause atherosclerosis, and unsaturated fats, such as vegetable oils, are safer than animal (saturated) fats; soft margarine is better than butter or hard margarine. Fibre in the diet is thought to guard against heart disease.

High blood pressure (or hypertension) increases with age, and can lead to heart attacks, strokes and kidney disease. If you have a Caribbean or African background you may be susceptible to high blood pressure and to diabetes, but less so to heart disease.

Following a low-fat, low-salt diet and increasing the daily intake of fibre is a necessary part of life for anyone with heart disease or high blood pressure. Exercise may sound like a bad idea, but in fact it will do good: raising the pulse rate to 120 beats per minute each day for two minutes, and exercising the whole body fully is the recommended regime. A gentle form of exercise, such as

Yoga and Tai Chi, will also increase ability to relax – an effective way of coping with conditions such a high blood pressure.

The idea of doing relaxation exercises may sound unnecessary, but they can make all the difference. You can teach yourself at home, through books or cassettes, or attend classes. Alternatively, you can switch off by listening to music, or think about something peaceful.

Adult education authorities hold day and evening classes in relaxation (movement, breathing and mental relaxation); and some are designed especially for women or older people. Your doctor should know if local hospitals or health centres run relaxation classes – or the library may have information about classes run by 'natural health' centres. The organisation Relaxation for Living offers cassettes and classes, in some areas of the country.

For smokers only

What doctors say is unfortunately true: smoking can lead to cancer and to serious heart and lung diseases such as emphysema and bronchitis. But giving up will immediately reduce the risk of heart disease, and circulation problems can improve within just weeks. Eventually the chances of developing lung cancer and other diseases will also be lessened, until they are the same as for non-smokers.

If you are determined to give up smoking, you are already off to a good start. You may be able give up gradually, or decide one day to remove everything connected with smoking from your house - and give up from that day on. Work out the times of day when the desire for a cigarette is most likely to undermine your good intentions, and be prepared. Do something with your hands, tapestry work or knitting, change your daily routine or try relaxation exercises. Many people have found it has helped to make a pact with a friend who is also giving up; or they have asked for sponsorship from their friends, fellow office workers or family (their support will be invaluable). And you can line up a special treat to celebrate when the battle is won – using the money that has been saved on a holiday or to buy yourself something special.

Taking a health check

There are a number of health aspects worth checking on from middle age onwards; some may already be a long-standing habit that should be kept up.

Cervical smear test

Ideally you will have been having regular cervical smear tests every two years – if so, continue till the age of 65, provided the last two tests have shown negative results. After that you will not need to have any more smears taken. However, there are many older women who have not had regular testing, and if you are one of these, it is important that you have tests done.

You can go to your doctor for a smear test, but if yours does not do them, or you prefer to go to a doctor you don't know so well, or would rather see a woman doctor, you can make an appointment at the family planning clinic or well-woman clinic, if there is one in your area. These are normally held in health clinics, on regular days each month – perhaps two sessions each month. If there is no well-woman clinic, the family planning clinic will also do smear tests, often on special cytology clinic days. You can find out where the clinics are held from your local area health authority (in the telephone directory).

Breast examination

To detect early signs of cancer, this is especially important for the over-50s. Self-examination should be done every month, but the first step is to go to a doctor, or to a health centre, to be taught how to do it. A leaflet explaining what to do should be given to you then, or you can get one from the Women's National Cancer Control Campaign (address on page 152)

Under the NHS mammography screening programme, any woman over 40 can go to her doctor and ask to be referred for a mammogram. If your doctor does refer you automatically, don't assume that there is something wrong – it may be that you have lumpy breasts which are more easily examined by a mammogram. As a further safety check, your GP may refer you if there is a family history of breast cancer.

Blood pressure

If you are overweight, or have a family history of high blood pressure, your blood pressure should be checked once a year. The doctor should, in any case, check regularly those who have heart or kidney disease, or diabetes, or have suffered a stroke.

Eyesight

It is normal to be wearing glasses for reading by about 50, and eyes should be checked by an optician every two years. The NHS allows a free examination every year. If there is any pain or redness, or difficulty in seeing, visit an optician as soon as possible.

One of the conditions that can be detected through screening long before you notice any symptoms is glaucoma, when the pressure of the fluid increases inside the eyeball. Glaucoma can be treated with eye drops or tablets, but if left too late does irreparable damage. So you need a screening when the eyes get their two-yearly test.

Cataract (clouding of the lens of the eye) may also be detected by the optician rather earlier than you may notice a worsening of your ability to see clearly. The cataract can be treated either with spectacles and advice about home lighting, or sometimes with an operation.

Teeth and gums

Nobody wants false teeth, so the way to avoid them is to keep gums in good condition and prevent decay round the base of the teeth. Use a narrow-headed brush like the 'Interspacer', for working round the gum line after using an ordinary toothbrush, or work between the teeth with dental floss. Don't worry if there is bleeding – it simply means you are dislodging any food deposits and helping the gums to become tighter.

Sugary foods, including soft drinks, play havoc with teeth, so choose pure fruit juices. Get a dental check every year. Dentures should be checked every three years so that they can be altered if necessary to allow for any changes in the shape of the gums.

Hearing

Although hearing can be expected to become less acute with age, if you cannot hear the telephone or a conversation against a low level of background noise, you should talk to your doctor. The problem may simply be wax in the ear, but it may need the attention of a specialist at the ear, nose and throat (ENT) department of the hospital. If a hearing aid is necessary, it is important to make sure that the aid fits properly – if there is any difficulty, go back to the ENT department for further advice and help. Don't be embarrassed about wearing an aid which may not be noticeable to other people and ensures you do not become cut off from family and social life.

If you are hard of hearing, your family and friends can help by speaking slowly and clearly (rather than loudly) and you can help yourself by going to lip-reading classes; there may be one at a local adult education college or centre for the deaf and hard of hearing.

Healthy feet

If you've worn high heels a great deal, you may by now be finding that the ball of your foot has spread to take the extra weight, and you need a broader fitting shoe. It is worth shopping around to find ones that fit properly so that you don't find your activities restricted by painful feet later on. Also, of course, it is no good having well-fitting shoes if your toes continue to be cramped by tights or socks (even bedsocks). Bedroom slippers are not really suitable for wearing for long periods, because they do not support the feet. Good support is also vital in the shoes you wear for exercise, whether it be walking or playing tennis; specially designed exercise footwear, such as track shoes, will ensure comfortable feet and are worth investing in.

Looking after the skin of your feet pays off, too – dry gently but thoroughly after washing (at least once a day) using plenty of talcum powder afterwards. Toenails should be cut regularly and straight across. The skin of the feet of people with diabetes or circulatory disease does not heal as quickly as it should, so they will need to have toenails cut, and cuts and abrasions dealt with by a chiropodist.

Chiropody is available through the NHS, though the service is very overstretched. Those with special needs, including the elderly, will be referred through their GP. If your feet need the special treatment that only a qualified chiropodist can give (if they are painful, or if you suffer from corns), but you do not qualify as a 'high priority' case for NHS treatment, you may have to go to a chiropodist privately, choosing one with SRCh (State Registered Chiropodist) after the name. A list is available from the Society of Chiropodists (address on page 151).

Talking to the doctor

Some doctors have a reputation for being dismissive of older women. They do not seem to have time to talk, or are inclined to dismiss symptoms with an 'it's just your age' attitude. Naturally, this has the effect of making some women hesitant about going to the surgery, reluctant to waste the doctor's time and over-conscious of the queue in the waiting-room. No wonder 'alternative' medicines are considered to be more successful than conventional ones, as the practitioners generally have more time to spend in discussing a patient's problems!

It helps if you do some preparation work before seeing the doctor. Write down all the questions you want to ask and don't quite dare, and also make a note of any medication already being taken, before going to the surgery. If there is a special test to be done, tell the receptionist in advance, so that more time can be allocated if necessary. Wearing easily removable clothing helps if there is likely to be a physical examination.

A blank piece of paper and pencil will come in useful in the surgery, too – for writing down the doctor's advice on treatment and the dosage of any prescription that may be given. Remember to ask about possible side effects (some drugs, for instance, interfere with vitamin absorption so that vitamin supplements may be necessary). A pharmacist, too, will be able to advise on dosage. The book *Know Your Medicines*, also published by Age Concern England, gives useful information on when to take drugs and their possible side effects.

Sometimes a little self-assertiveness may be needed if you feel you are getting nowhere with your carefully prepared questions. Don't get into an argument or make any accusations. Simply repeat your question, point out that you would like an informative answer. Insist on a second opinion, if necessary.

If you have problems speaking English, take an interpreter with you; either a friend or a trained interpreter who will be able to put questions across to the doctor without being talked down to (which can happen). There are expensive, private interpreting agencies, and voluntary ones in areas with a large number of people from ethnic minorities – contact your local Community Relations Council. Unfortunately, not all doctors and hospital staff are sensitive to cultural differences and fully aware of the shyness of women who may be very reluctant to undergo a physical examination.

The taking of medicines and pills can produce almost as many problems as they solve if doctors do not take enough care over ensuring that we as patients understand how much and how frequently the medication should be taken, especially if there are several different types. A pill timetable, which allows each one to be crossed off as it is taken, could help. Often repeat prescriptions are issued without the doctor seeing the patient, or taking into account the fact that as people get older they have increased pharmacological sensitivity. Drug overprescribing can occur when patients are discharged from hospital with a supply of medicines, which are duplicated by the GP.

Women are prescribed more tranquillisers and mood changing drugs than men, for conditions such as depression, perhaps following bereavement, stress or anxiety. They can be very useful in the short term, but there should be close cooperation with the doctor so they should be given up as soon as possible. Many of the admissions to geriatric wards are thought to be drug induced – as many as 10 to 15 per cent with the sleeping pill Mogadon, a particular sinner. However, antidepressants are sometimes life-savers, and so these and some of the other drugs that are used in treating mental illness should not be given up suddenly or without a doctor's support.

If you want to avoid drugs and need someone to talk to about emotional problems, there are various agencies to help. Some cities have women's counselling and therapy centres, which offer individual and group psychotherapy sessions and workshops (address on page 147). There may be a drop-in time when someone going through a short-term crisis can attend informally, perhaps just to talk over problems with an unbiased, trained counsellor. More often there are workshops which cover topics such as drug dependency, compulsive eating, sexuality. There are also agencies offering counselling, as listed on page 156.

It is possible to get psychotherapy through the NHS, but waiting lists are very long. Your doctor can refer you to a hospital psychiatric clinic where drugs may or may not be prescribed and where you may be referred on for psychotherapy. Whereas psychiatrists treat mental illness, the role of the psychotherapist is to help normal but unhappy people to enjoy happier lives.

Obviously you throw away (or, preferably, take back to the pharmacist) any drugs no longer needed. Never try other people's medication and tell the doctor of any other drugs you may be taking: whether they are proprietary medicines from the chemist or those prescribed by an 'alternative' consultant. It is not always easy to 'confess' to alternative treatment or to having consulted an alternative practitioner; and in many cases you can expect a less-than-enthusiastic response from the average conventional GP. But it is only fair to tell all – we have to communicate with our doctors if we want them to communicate with us!

Further reading

Better Health in Retirement
  Dr J A Muir Gray, Age Concern England, 1982

Eat Well, Stay Well and
Eat Well, Stay Well for Afro-Caribbeans
  Age Concern Greater London

Eating Well on a Budget
  BBC Food & Drink Progamme, Age Concern England, 1987

Cystitis: Complete Self-help Guide
  Angela Kilmartin, Hamlyn, 1985

Menopause, A Positive Approach
  Rosetta Reitz, Allen and Unwin, 1985

Natural Health in Gynaecology
  Rita Nissin, Pandora, 1986

The Prime of Your Life
   Dr Miriam Stoppard, Penguin, 1986

Know Your Medicines
   Pat Blair, Age Concern England, 1985

Trouble with Tranqillisers
   MIND, 1982, address on page 151

More Easy Cooking for One or Two
   Louise Davies, Penguin, 1979

Dental Care in Retirement (Factsheet)
   Age Concern England. Free with SAE

Breaking the Sound Barrier; Information for Older Hearing Impaired People
   Royal Institute for the Deaf, address on page 151

Feeling good, looking good Caroline Dudley discusses how to improve your pleasure in life as well as your appearance

---

*F*eeling good and looking good are closely related. If we feel confident about ourselves, this radiates into our approach to life and people, and makes us look good too. It's a sign that we like ourselves and enjoy being alive. The effect of good posture is an immediate example of this. If we stand straight and look the world in the eye, we actually feel better able to cope, whereas if we slouch around feeling old and crumpled, we feel more easily put upon, and indeed the world will more easily put-upon us.

Looking good means different things to different people. For many it means a desire to look younger than our years, to postpone the wrinkles, the loss of contour, and thus to gain 'approval' from those around us. Ironically, a marked desire for approval by others is the least beautifying attitude around, and when we regard those older women whom we perceive as beautiful, we find that their beauty, although possibly enhanced by a good complexion and expensive clothes, stems in reality from an inner confidence and pleasure in life. This is true of women at any age.

For this reason, this chapter looks at the outer woman and also the inner one. The first part is about gaining confidence and having a new outlook on life, the second about beauty care and appearance.

Believing in yourself

Feeling good means being out there in the world, broadening horizons, interacting with other people of all ages, having the confidence to voice your needs and being prepared to acknowledge those of others. Retirement provides an unique opportunity for all this. It gives us time to re-examine our lives, and ourselves, and become the woman we really want to be.

But for some, it's not easy. Acquiring confidence isn't something we can do overnight. And since age is neither respected not revered, it can be difficult to feel that one's view is welcomed, one's presence wanted. Gaining the confidence to walk tall is, however, within our grasp. There are, for instance, groups and courses arising out of the women's movement that provide an opportunity for personal growth and exploration – women can share their experiences in creative writing, in assertiveness training, or even about entering public life.

Assertiveness training

This set of techiques can teach you to put your point of view forward firmly and calmly, without resorting to manipulative tactics such as weeping, sulking or acting like a martyr. Women, traditionally conditioned to put the needs of others before their own, can find that assertiveness training helps to dispel some well-tried myths, such as: the need for your behaviour to be approved of by others; the belief that we cannot change our attitudes to life, even if they are stifling us; and the idea that guilt and worry are an indication of humaneness and will change the way things are.

Then there are other issues to be questioned: that you do not have the right to fail at anything; that there is an absolute system of right and wrong; that you have to live by the 'ought' and 'should' syndrome; that you need psychological dependence and have to take responsibility for others; that you have no control over your emotions, especially anger, and that you are not worthy.

In contrast, the list of assertive rights reads like a freedom charter, which in many ways it is. It allows you to see yourself as a responsible person, who is worthy of consideration. You have the right to: judge your own behaviour, thoughts and emotions, and to take responsibility for their initiation and consequences; to offer no excuses or reasons to justify your behaviour; to change your mind; to make mistakes and be responsible for them; to say 'I don't know', 'I don't understand'; to be independent of the goodwill of others.

Using these assertive rights may require a fundamental rethink of your way of relating to others and to yourself, and the classes teach certain techniques to help achieve this. Of course they are not going to transform a quiet person into an aggressive one, or, for that matter, an aggressive person into a passive one, but they can help you to see more clearly your own weaknesses and those of others. The instances in which assertive techniques are useful range from coping with situations where no close emotional relationship is involved, like returning faulty goods to a store and asking for a refund, to marking out your own space in a relationship, or making your sexual requirements known to your partner.

Make no mistake, assertiveness training may come as a surprise to your nearest and dearest, because however assertive you are naturally, your way of dealing with situations and conflicts will change, either radically or subtly, and can make others, especially spouses and children, who are not changing in the same way, feel deeply threatened. As one woman said, after attending a self-assertiveness course as part of a management training scheme:

《 For the first time, I feel as though I know who I am, because I'm not afraid to state what I want. At first, my husband was rather shocked, and it took him a while to get used to the new, more straightforward me. But we worked through it and now, after a couple of years, I feel it has strengthened our relationship. 》

Details of courses nationwide, which usually consist of six to ten two-hour sessions, are available from the Redwood Women's Training Association. Another association, Skills with People, also run courses for groups of ten to twelve; and if you can form a group of this size, a course – lasting one, two or three days – can be tailor-made for your requirements (addresses on page 144). Local authorities also run assertiveness training courses as part of their adult education programmes. Although several excellent books are available, from which the techniques can be learned, the best plan is to join a class, where you can do the practical exercises.

Broadening your horizons

If you regard retirement as an opportunity for further study or to pursue a recently acquired interest, a Fresh Horizons course may be for you. They are run by local adult education authorities, and in some areas are known as Fresh Start, Return to Study, Access or Breakthrough. Preference is given to older women applicants, and the courses form a gateway to higher education, with 70 per cent of students going on to universities and polytechnics.

To start with, you select a package, which might consist of, say, study skills, sociology, history, maths and literature, and in the second term you can take another option, perhaps specialising in a certain area of study. These courses, although open to both men and women, are primarily designed to suit women, both by the timing of classes and choice of subject matter, which takes a woman's perspective of sociology and literature.

The courses last from three weeks, for a 'taster' course, ideal to see if you will enjoy the discipline of academic work, to a year, and attendance can be part-time day or evening, or full-time during the day, which is four days a week. For further information contact your local educational advice centre, through the town hall.

Developing your social life

If you're hoping to develop a more fulfilling social life in retirement, there are many women's organisations offering activities, new interests, an opportunity to meet women from many walks of life, and a warm welcome. One of the best known of these is the Women's Institute. Though essentially a countrywomen's organisation, members may participate in both country and national events and attend the residential college at Denham, near Abingdon. For women in Scotland and Northern Ireland there are national counterparts.

The Townswomen's Guild is a similar organisation designed to meet the needs of town-based women. Its programmes include drama, music, lectures, teach-ins on money, health and beauty courses, sports and leisure.

The Mother's Union, which welcomes members of all denominations, is a worldwide society, whose main objective is to advance the Christian religion. It is deeply concerned with issues of marriage and the family and provides holidays for families under stress. The National Women's Register consists of a network of groups of women who meet at each other's houses for stimulating and wide-ranging discussions in response to the requests of local membership such as learning to play bridge or a book reading group. They also organise outings and activities. See addresses on pages 156-8.

Some councils fund women's centres, and you can get the address and opening times from the council as well as the library and your local newspaper, which are also are good sources of information about what's going on in your community. One activity that has proved very popular at women's centres is creative writing. With the comforting support of an all-women group, many women have taken their first tentative steps at writing, perhaps short stories, reminiscences from childhood, plays, or poetry, and have gained fulfilment from exploring these latent talents.

Women's centres also often have a 'drop-in' time, where you can meet others for coffee and a chat, and at other times visiting speakers address the group on issues affecting women, followed by informal discussion. Some have meetings on health, the menopause, and offer a chance to exchange views on personal experiences.

In London the Older Feminists Network keeps in touch with members via a newsletter, and aims to form pressure groups on issues including health, housing and transport for older women. The newly opened Wesley House, Women's Centre, near Holborn in Central London forms a base for many different activities (addresses on page 158). Pensioners Link (formerly known as Task Force) is another London based group with centres in different areas which believes in the rights of pensioners to live independent and active lives; and among its activities offers an advisory service about people's queries relating to pensions and benefits (address on page 155).

Campaigning for something

Working for a cause is both satisfying and provides an opportunity to meet people and increase confidence. There are many groups of women, all over the country, campaigning for a better deal in our society. These groups could do with your support. After all, we constitute 52 per cent of the population, but this fact is not related in the numbers of women in politics, in top management jobs and other influential positions.

If there is something about the present status of women that strikes you as unfair, such as the archaic tax laws, the use of women as sex objects in advertisements, lack of management training for women; the difficulties experienced by women returning to the job market; or inadequate funding of well-woman projects, remember there are plenty of issues to be tackled now that you have the time and the energy to help.

One organisation which campaigns on a variety of issues, such as tax laws, health, education and equality between the sexes is the Fawcett Society, founded in 1866, whose early members were instrumental in getting the vote for women (address on page 157). Members are of all ages, from young professional women to the retired, and meetings are held in central London.

If you feel the way forward for women's equality is to have more women in Parliament, then there's the 300 Group, whose aims are to encourage women of all races and democratic political beliefs to stand for Parliament, the European Parliament and local councils. The group holds workshops, discussions and debates on important topics and has local branches in England, Scotland and Wales (address on page 158).

Many women are committed to pressure groups concerned with racism, environmental protection, nuclear disarmament, to name but a few of the current ones. Throughout this book and in the 'Directory of useful organisations' there are groups listed that may seem particularly relevant to your interests.

For appearance' sake

Not all women pay a great deal of attention to beauty care or fashion. It may be through personal preference – to some it can seem a waste of time and very superficial. Or it may be through a political principle. Many feminists feel that to make themselves artificially attractive turns them into sex objects in men's eyes. Some make a point of always wearing trousers, never a dress or skirt.

But many women find buying new clothes and trying new make-up stimulating and fun. If when over 50 they lack confidence in choosing and applying make-up, clothes and hairstyles, this is hardly surprising. We receive little enough coverage in fashion and beauty magazines. It is as though we cease to exist after age 40. We have no role models in the media to which we can relate, as one 60-year-old woman confirmed:

《 *I've given up having magazines delivered because they are just not geared to the older woman. We too are interested in clothes, make-up and hairstyles. Because we are frightened of looking like the proverbial mutton dressed as lamb, we tend to go entirely the other way and not be adventurous enough.* 》

Basic skin care

Apart from the expensive creams, which claim to postpone wrinkling, there seems to be a dearth of skin care products or make-up aimed specifically at the older women's market. Expensive products with extravagant claims do not stand up to the rigorous tests of scientists, who find no evidence of skin regeneration through special oils, hormones, vitamins or other substances. The fact is, skin as it ages loses both moisture and also the basic fibrous support system which makes it firm and plump. Gradually it wrinkles and loses elasticity – more on the face and hands than anywhere else because these are the areas most exposed to the drying effects of wind and heat and the unkind rays of the sun. To keep skin in reasonable condition, the old routine helps: cleanse, tone and nourish, albeit with emphasis on the nourishment, bearing in mind the limitations of all beauty products.

Little of the nourishment applied to the skin actually penetrates, and the most you can do is keep the surface smooth and reasonably moist. Apply moisturiser under make-up for daytime. Use night cream, which contains more oils and less moisture, just before going to bed, for a richer protection. Don't choose anything very thick and heavy, as it can make the skin feel clogged and greasy, and even have a dragging effect. Always apply any cream or lotion with a very gently upward movement – so as not to encourage sagging – and be careful around the eyes.

The St Michael fragrance-free range of skin care products, available from Marks and Spencer, represents good value for money, as do the Body Shop products. For a touch of luxury if your skin is very dry, try Dr Payot's Hydriane, which is exceptionally rich in moisture, or Revlon's European Collagen Complex, a rich, light cream, which can be used during the day, under make-up and at night.

Two anti-ageing products, albeit pricey ones, which have proved effective are Capture, by Christian Dior and the Niosome system, by Lancome. Capture (£39 for 30 ml) used night and morning under moisturiser softens wrinkles by plumping up the cells on either side of them, while Niosome (£13.95 for 30 ml) works on the principle of slowing down intercellular deterioration.

Cleansing the skin means removing make-up and any surface grime. One of the advantages of older skins is that they are not greasy and not prone to the septic spots of adolescence. So a light cream or lotion is all that is necessary. Ideally, don't apply soap and water on the face at all, but if you must occasionally, use a superfatted soap and rinse thoroughly.

Toning sounds like a good idea, but can be a nasty experience for older skins. Many toners are astringent, and contain alcohol – far too drying. So when choosing one, check the label and buy a toner that states it is suitable for dry or delicate skins. Apply after you have finished cleansing, to remove the last traces of stale make-up and cleanser.

If you feel you'd like to try a face pack, avoid clay-type products as they, too, are drying, and go instead for a creamy one such as Elizabeth Arden's Velva Cream Pack, which claims to cleanse the skin of deep-seated grime, and to nourish it simultaneously. But remember, deep-cleansing is more myth than necessity.

There are ways to protect skin and reduce the effects of sun and wind. When selecting a sunblock, which you should use religiously against the wrinkling effects of the sun, choose a higher protection factor than you have in former years. A protection factor higher than 6 is recommended for any skin exposed to the sun, to guard against skin cancer. Uvistat Sun Screen High Protection Factor 10 which can be worn under make-up, or Supatan Sun Block, both give high protection.

Research carried out in the United States has shown that smokers are prone to more and deeper wrinkles than non-smokers, and develop them at an earlier age. In the tests, the complexions of smokers in the 40 to 49 age group compared badly with non-smokers twenty years their senior. These differences can result from smoking ten or more cigarettes a day for fifteen years, and even ex-smoking men and women in their 40s, who had given up smoking in their teens and 20s had excessively wrinkled skin. However, no matter when you stop smoking, one of the immediate benefits is that your skin will look clearer and fresher within days.

Albert Kligman, Professor of Dermatology at the University of Pennsylvania School of Medicine, believes that we can keep our skins wrinkle-free, or at least stop deterioration, by using petroleum jelly for daily skin care. He recommends that the following routine should be maintained for life (preferably starting in childhood!): Take a good blob of petroleum jelly on the fingertips of both hands and massage it into clean skin with gentle, circular movements. You must do this for one minute, then take a tissue and wipe off the excess, so that what is left lodges in the skin's tiny crevices.

Whether you can be bothered to follow Kligman's scheme is a personal matter, whether it works perhaps depends as much on faith as anything else. But it is certainly cheaper than most skin regeneration creams.

To protect your hands at night, use a heavy handcream, such as Glycinello or Codella. If your hands are cracked or very dry, put the cream on thickly, covered by a pair of cotton gloves, so that it can continue to act while you sleep. If you suffer from splitting nails and dry cuticles, use clippers to keep your nails short, and, with a fine emery board, shape them into a rounded rather than a pointed contour, so that the side of the nail has sufficient support.

Updating your make-up

Not everyone ignores the make-up requirements of older women. One expert on the subject in London is Edwina Payne, tutor of beauty therapists at Joan Price's Face Place (address on page 144). Her students, once qualified, give a total of 8,000 lessons a year to older women who want to update their make-up techniques. The lessons are particularly popular because older women can't find out how to make up by looking in magazines, and they need help to find out how to adapt the current trends to their own age group.

As with nourishing creams, you can spend a fortune on make-up if you have the money and inclination, and the 'placebo' factor may make the effect seem worth it. But remember that the main difference between the cheap and expensive brands is that the price of the dearer ones incorporates an enormous amount for packaging and advertising. Popular, cheaper brands of cosmetics are well tested and no more likely to harm your skin, unless you have an allergy, in which case choose from a hypo-allergenic range, such as Almay or Clinique.

It is possible that the more expensive brands may be more thoroughly refined, although this is by no means certain, and are more likely to hold their colour fastness better. They also offer a larger and more subtle range of colours. Edwina's advice to those on a budget is to buy an expensive foundation cream, as that is the most important item, and take the trouble to see that the colour is just right for your skin. Then you can get away with less expensive eye make-up if you have to.

When applying make-up there are several ways to minimise the presence of wrinkles:

● Use a light textured foundation, very sparingly, making sure you blend it in well around the jawline, to avoid a mask-line effect.

Fix it with loose powder, rather than the compressed type. A matt powder is better for this purpose than one with a sheen. Use very little, and brush off any surplus. Some older women say they prefer a very light coating of a matt foundation and no powder. Tissue off any surplus. The last thing you want is a powdery or heavy 'pancake' look.

- Use a matt eye shadow. The frosted, iridescent type accentuates creases. Instead of light blues and greens, consider 'pigment' colours such as brown, taupe or plum, as these tend to look more natural.

- When applying mascara, make sure that all the lashes are separated and not stuck together in clumps. When lashes become sparser, this is particularly important. The best way to conceal the sparseness of lashes is to have them dyed, but this must be professionally done, as the dye must not come into contact with the eye itself. This costs around £5.50, takes about half an hour, and lasts for six to eight weeks.

- Pencil in eyebrows, using short, feathery strokes, with a brown or grey pencil; avoid using black pencil eye-liner unless your natural colouring is very dark.

- In applying lipstick, to reduce the 'spidery' effect of the little 'up' lines around the lips, outline the lips with a lip pencil, then apply lipstick, not from the stick itself, but with a lip brush, inside the outline, avoiding the corners of the mouth. Choose soft, gentle lip colours, dark rather than pale. Gloss lipsticks are fine as long as the colour is muted.

- When choosing blusher, avoid the rouge-based type as they are based on grease and do not create a natural effect. There are fine powdered blushers and also lotion types to smooth on with a finger. Clinique make a lotion blusher, which is easy to apply and gives a natural effect without greasiness. Apply powdered blusher very carefully with a piece of cotton wool or bristle brush. The nylon brushes supplied with some blushers can make a hard line.

- Finally, take a good look, with glasses on, if you use them, to see that there are no hard lines. Eyeliner and shadow should be smudged and soft.

Controlling unwanted hair

It is an incontrovertible fact that we get hairier as we get older, and the image of women unblemished, hairless as babies, is a fantasy of man and the advertising industry. Nevertheless, hair on a woman's face is always unwanted and unwelcome – no matter what her age.

If there are only a few hairs, they can be removed with tweezers, but remember that when re-growth occurs, the hairs are stronger. Waxing can be effective, especially for a shadow on the upper lip, but this should be done professionally with warm wax, rather than the cold wax strips sold for home use. The effectiveness of waxing depends on the wax being pulled off swiftly, and this is very difficult to do on yourself. If you choose a depilatory cream, make sure it is formulated for the face: the creams sold for underarms and legs are too strong, and can 'burn' the skin, making it sore.

The only permanent means of removing unwanted hair is by electrolysis. An electric current is passed through a needle into the hair follicle and burns off the hair root. Although not painful, the heat of the needle does cause slight discomfort. A course of from six to twelve half-hour sessions is usual, spaced over a period of a year, and although during this time there may be some re-growth, when these hairs have been removed, the effect is usually permanent. Go to a trained member of the Institute of Electrolysis (address on page 145) at a beauty salon. Some practitioners come to you at home. A half-hour session of electrolysis will cost around £10.00.

A new innovation, using a similar technique, is Depilex. In this treatment the electric current is passed through a pair of tweezers to the hair, which is then lifted out of the hair follicle. It can also handle curly hairs, which are difficult to treat by electrolysis, and causes less discomfort. It is slightly cheaper but there is more chance of regrowth than with electrolysis. Legs and, if you wish, underarms can be de-fuzzed by waxing or depilatory creams, and re-growth takes about six weeks. Shaving is the tried and tested answer, but it has the disadvantages that you may nick your skin, and stubble regrows in a couple of days.

Other facial treatments

Nothing will keep a face looking young forever. But there are special teatments which claim to make you look younger and more beautiful, though rarely do you see claims to restoring elasticity, eliminating wrinkles, removing deep lines and improving contours. However, if you feel better after a beauty treatment, the chances are you will look better. Again, whether you do so as a result of the treatment itself or because of the pampering and indulgence implicit in the treatment is anybody's guess. The treatments described in this section are pricey and may seem highly unnecessary and undesirable to some people, but they are included as factual information.

One treatment, suitable for older skins, and developed in France by Rene Guinot, is cathiodermie. This is like the Rolls Royce of facials. In addition to its deep cleansing function, it uses galvanic and high frequency currents to boost circulation, preparing the skin to receive the nourishing creams, which, it is claimed, are absorbed more deeply into the skin, thus prolonging the youth of the tissue and postponing wrinkling. A treatment takes $1\frac{1}{2}$ hours.

Bio-peeling is another treatment, which aims to restore a youthful feel to the skin, without surgery, but it is not recommended for older skins. Some years ago, the use of cold-beam laser treatment caused a brief flurry of excitement, as it claimed to smooth out lines and depressions, but this was never proven.

To lift or not to lift?

This is the most drastic of anti-wrinkle treatments: surgery. In an ideal world we would be more accepting of ourselves, wrinkles and all, believing in the dignity of growing older, and even being regarded by others as deserving of respect for our experience and wisdom, not to mention our wrinkles. But until that day dawns, some of us will want to resort to surgery to restore the contours.

Having decided that you do want, and can afford to have, a face lift of some kind, the best way to approach it is via your GP. Explain what you want done, and ask him or her to recommend a surgeon. Alternatively, you may know someone who has had this type of surgery and has been happy with it. In any case, treat advertisements for cosmetic surgery with the greatest care. The advertisements will probably say that all the surgeons they

recommend are 'fully qualified'. They may well be Fellows of the
Royal College of Surgeons, but, more to the point, what is their
speciality? You don't want a surgeon qualified in orthopaedics.
Having got the name of a bona fide cosmetic surgeon, find out
where he or she works most of the time – preferably at a teaching
hospital – and make your own enquiries as to the type of work
generally undertaken.

The most often requested, and most successful, type of cosmetic
surgery is blepharoplasty, to remove under-eye bags and reshape
eyelids. This will require three days in hospital and will cost
around £800. The stitches will be removed 48 hours later, and
complete recovery should be achieved in three months. A full face
lift, for which incisions are made in front of and behind the ears
and hidden in the hairline, requires the same length of hospital
stay, but will cost around £1,500. Some stitches are removed after
five to seven days, the rest after two weeks, during which time the
patient should convalesce. The swelling goes down after four
weeks, and the effect of this operation should last eight years. You
cannot have more than one or two repeats in later years. For more
information on cosmetic surgery, contact the Alternative and
Orthodox Medicine Clinic (address on page 144).

Hair care and colour

As at any age, it's the cut that makes the difference as to whether
your hair looks most becoming. A new hairstyle is one of the
quickest ways of creating a new image – though it does take some
nerve. Play around with pins to see the effect, and discuss it with
your hairdresser. Some styles need more 'body' than others, and
you have to find something that suits your hair as well as your face.
On the whole, older faces benefit from softer styles that frame the
face rather than severe lines. Even if you have good cheekbones,
there's the jawline that may need softening.

As with the skin, the oils in the scalp will decrease somewhat, so
use a richer shampoo and/or conditioner. Hair, seen in close-up, is
covered by tiny 'scales', and conditioner smoothes these down,
making the hair less prone to tangling, and protecting it from
damage by brushing and combing. There are confusing varieties of
shampoos to choose from, some of which are harsher than others,
and some more suitable for certain types of hair. You could cut

down on the chances of error by asking your hairdresser for an analysis of your hair and scalp. He or she is likely to recommend a product stocked by the salon, which is usually more expensive than products sold in chemists. A good product available only from hairdressers is shampoo combined with conditioner from the Wella System Professional range. From chemists, the best brands are those made by manufacturers who also supply hairdressers, such as Wella, L'Oreal, etc. Instead of setting lotions, which have a high alcohol content, or heavy sprays and lacquers, try using one of the mousses now available, which will have a less drying effect.

If you are thinking of having a perm, it is best to have it done professionally. Many hairdressers offer reduced prices for pensioners early in the week. Make a preliminary visit to discuss your requirements, and make sure that the stylist understands what you want, and can recommend the right type of perm for your particular hair. Healthy hair has an acid coating, which is easily stripped through the use of harsh shampoos, colourants and perms. When this happens, it's rather like an apple that has lost its peel – also acid-based. The apple browns and wrinkles, losing its quality. Hair responds in a similar way, so perms and other hair products should have what hairdressers call an 'acid balance'. L'Oreal make an acid-balance perm, which claims to be non-alkaline.

Colouring is something you can try at home; and if you've had a perm, wait until at least six weeks after the perm to colour or add highlights . The old 'blue rinse' – or for that matter, lilac rinse – are not to many people's taste today, but if you want to make the most of your elegant grey hair, there are various temporary colourants you might like to try, including Inecto Hint of a Tint and Wella Colour Set, which offer several shades of grey. If your hair is just beginning to turn grey, how about emphasising it with silver highlights? These are difficult to do at home, so best consult your hairdresser.

For those of us who lack the courage or inclination to let the grey hairs show, there is a great range of colourants for use at home. But results can be uneven, especially when there are only a few grey hairs, as these are wiry and colour-resistant. When hair has turned completely grey, it usually regains its softer texture and becomes easier to colour. To try a new colour without committing yourself too much, use a 'temporary' hair colourant, which will wash out at the next wash.

If you want the colour to last through four to six washes, go for a semi-permanent type, and for the kind that stays until it grows out, use a 'permanent' colourant. This last type is potentially more damaging to the hair as it penetrates the hair shaft, rather than just coating it with colour. One product designed to conceal grey hair is Loving Care, a semi-permanent colourant. It comes in 20 colours and covers any amount of grey. For a natural effect, choose the shade nearest to your original colour. Steer clear of metallic dyes which claim to make your hair get darker gradually. These products do darken hair over a period of weeks, but you can't repeat the process, or have a perm, until it grows out, which can leave you with a patchy effect.

Other factors, too, can leave you with a hair colour other than what you had in mind: sun, salt and chlorine can lift the colour of hair, or bleach it, so be sure to shower with fresh water after swimming. If you are taking any drugs, steroids, or undergoing radiation therapy, these treatments can make hair colour resistant. Be sure to tell your hairdresser so that he or she can compensate by altering the dilutions or timing of the colourant if necessary.

Clothing your image

Now that you are embarking on a new phase of life, and moving in a new direction, you have a great opportunity to express yourself in the way you dress.

The single most liberating influence on women's fashion in recent years has been the tracksuit. Where previously older women wore day dresses and unadventurous separates, leaving flamboyant colours and impetuous styles strictly to the young, now the gap has narrowed, and older women are allowing themselves more freedom, taking advantage of the casual wear so fashionable today.

Those who became fashion-conscious just after the war will have inherited a respect for well-cut, well-made clothes, and a desire to look neat even if unremarkable. But this striving for bandbox neatness did not give women permission to dress with verve, and some women approaching retirement today want to redefine their approach to fashion, while lacking the tradition of confidence to do so.

The freer outlook took root in the 1960s, when fashion became available to all, clothes used cheap fabrics, were made on a shoestring, and sold at rock-bottom prices. Of course they lacked finish; but in their way, they had great style and flair, and made the better-made garments look matronly by contrast. The new styles were also more versatile and easier to mix and match to create new outfits. Although the prices are no longer rock-bottom, many of today's styles can be worn by women of all ages. If you can bear the loud pop music and the communal changing rooms of today's young fashion shops, you may well get a pleasant surprise at the range on offer.

One older woman, who dresses with great style and verve is Billie Figg, a freelance writer, who specialises in fashion, including styles for bigger sizes. She feels that too often women dress to disguise rather than for positive effect.

« *If someone wears muted colours because she likes and enjoys them, that's fine, but if she wears them because she is large and wants to be inconspicuous, that's the wrong reason. Being big and joyous is acceptable today, but being big and boring is unforgiveable.* »

If you do take a larger size, you can take advantage of big loose shirts and overtops, worn with a skirt or trousers. The great thing with trousers is that they give you a longer line in one colour. This also goes for the fashionable toning tights, elegant on anyone, but a special boon to larger women, and those with varicose veins.

Both for the sake of comfort and aesthetics, avoid buying clothes a size too small, and kidding yourself that you will diet to fit into them. If you try to squeeze into ill-fitting, skimpy clothes, you will destroy the line of the garment, and, incidentally, make yourself look fatter. Today's look is loose and languid, so don't keep buying the same dress size just because you've always bought it. One gem of wisdom dropped by Bruce Oldfield, who designs clothes for Princess Diana, is never to pull belts in too tight, as it just redistributes the bulges.

As to hemlines, Billie Figg emphasises that the last thing to do is choose 'just below the knee' because it's safe. Many older women could wear a hemline on the knee, midway down the calf or at the ankle. But Billie thinks women of 60 plus tend to look odd in micro-mini skirts, except, possibly for a short beach-dress on an older woman with unblemished veins.

She adds a note of hope about choices for older women in the larger size group though admitting that fashion designers find them less inspiring than youth and are not convinced that the older age group is economically viable. However, as the young women demand more styles in larger sizes, and designers cater for this need, older women will begin to see – at last – how to have fun in the way they dress.

If you are size 16 to 30, look out for a branch of Forgotten Woman opening near you. This chain has outlets in Loughton, Temple Fortune in North London, and Maidenhead, and many more are planned. Evans Collection, formerly Evans (Outsizes), has around 150 independent outlets throughout the country, plus fifty shops within Debenhams stores. Here sizes go from 14 to 30, and in some styles, up to size 36. As well as a comprehensive range of dresses, separates, lingerie, swimwear and coats, Evans also has accessories including larger sizes of hats and socks. When shopping at small boutiques, it's worth looking out for German manufacturers' labels, as they often include larger sizes in their ranges.

You will also find that several of the mail order catalogues feature stylish clothes in a wide range of sizes. Kays of Worcester offer excellent value, and mail order shopping has the advantage that payments can be made by instalments if cash is short for more expensive items.

A lot of older women who remain slim do thicken at the waist and below, as abdominal muscles weaken. This doesn't have to mean that anything with a waist is 'out'. Slim skirts and trousers work extremely well with loose, bloused tops belted at the waist or worn loose, perhaps half-buttoned like a jacket with a 'vest' top underneath. Dresses with skirts that are gently gathered at the waist so they fall loosely above and below can look good, as can dresses with a slightly raised or lowered waist, though voluminous smocks and caftans tend to look effective only when they are made in magnificent fabrics and you are the kind of person who can dress them up with dramatic jewellery. The line to avoid is anything that hugs the diaphragm and then stretches over the abdomen.

Accessories no longer need to match, and if you buy, say, a handbag that appeals to you in a bold colour, this can be teamed with shoes in a basic colour. Now that flat heels are in fashion, and if you find high heels uncomfortable, you can have up-to-the-minute footwear, in any price range, from the most expensive Italian calf to an effective mock patent from a chain store.

Once you've worked out all the accessories, your bold new fashion look will probably cause comment from those around you, and some of it may be less than approving. People like other people to be predictable. It reinforces their security. But it will also make your family and friends notice you, and realise that you are an individual who can function without their approval, not invisible, but a force to be reckoned with.

Further reading

Scientific Skin Care
David Murray, Arlington Books, 1985

Someone to Talk to Directory
Mental Health Foundation, 1985. See for reference at your library.

A Woman in Your Own Right
Anne Dickson, Quartet, 1982

Prime Time: The Mid-Life Woman in Focus
Helen Franks, Pan, 1981

A Way of Looking
Molton Brown, Ward Lock, 1987

Directory of useful organisations

grouped according to the subjects outlined below

Alternative medicine

Alternative and Orthodox Medicine Clinic
Information about treatments and therapies, also on cosmetic surgery.

PO Box 598
Harley House
Marylebone Road
London NW1 5HW
Tel: 01-486 7490/8087

British Homeopathic Association
For a list of practising GPs and pharmacies.

27a Devonshire Street
London W1N 1RJ
Tel:01-935 2165

British Naturopathic and Osteopathic Association

Address on page 150

General Council of Osteopaths

Address on page 151

National Institute of Medical Herbalists
For list of practising doctors and herbal suppliers.

Miss Janet Hicks
41 Hatherley Road
Winchester
Hampshire
Tel: 0962 68776

Assertiveness training

Redwood Women's Training Association
Runs courses, many available through local education authorities. Also offers women's sexuality workshops.

83 Fordwych Road
London NW2 3TL
Tel: 01-452 9261

Skills With People
Organises courses for groups of ten or more.

15 Liberia Road
London N5 1JP
Tel: 01-386 3605

Beauty therapy

Alternative and Orthodox Clinic

Address above

Joan Price's Face Place
Qualified beauty therapists give individual make-up lessons, using products from different ranges.

33 Cadogan Street
London SW3 2PP
Tel: 01-723 6671

Institute of Electrolysis
For list of qualified operators and
syllabus of training. Postal enquiries,
enclose SAE.

The Secretary
251 Seymour Grove
Manchester M16 ODS

Bereavement

CRUSE
Counselling, literature, local support
groups for bereaved people.

126 Sheen Road
Richmond
Surrey TW9 1UR
Tel: 01-940 4818

Gay Bereavement Project
Support and advice for bereavement of
a partner of the same sex.
(recorded message)
(duty volunteer)

Unitarian Rooms
Hoop Lane
London NW11 8BS
Tel: 01-455 8894
Tel: 01-837 7324

National Association for Widows
Advice, literature and local branches.
Also campaigns for widows' rights.

5 Chell Road
Stafford
ST16 5QA
Tel: 0785 45465

Carers support

Alzheimer's Disease Society
Advice, literature and local groups.

Bank Buildings
Fulham Broadway
London SW6 1EP
Tel: 01-381 3177

Arthritis Care

Address on page 151

Association of Carers
Advice, literature and self-help groups
for carers of disabled and/or elderly
people.

21-23 New Road
Chatham
Kent ME4 4QJ
Tel: 0634 813981

Chest, Heart and Stroke Association
Counselling, literature and local
groups.

Tavistock Ho. North
Tavistock Square
London WC1H 9JE
Tel: 01-387 3012

Crossroads (Association of Crossroads Care Attendant Schemes)
Provides trained home care for handicapped people.

Head Office
94 Cotton Road
Rugby
Warwickshire
CV21 3AQ
Tel: 0788 73653

Northern Ireland
87 University Street
Belfast BT7 1DL
Tel: 0232 231105

Scotland
24 George Square
Glasgow G2 1EG
Tel: 041-226 3793

Disabled Living Foundation
Extensive information on aids for disabled people.

384 Harrow Road
London W9 2HU
Tel: 01-289 6111

Disability Alliance
Provides advice and publishes annual rights handbook.

25 Denmark Street
London WC2H 8NS
Tel: 01-240 0806

Equal Opportunities Commission
Research and information about equal opportunities.

Overseas House
Quay Street
Manchester M3 3HN
Tel: 061-833 9244

Family Policy Studies Centre
Research and publications on aspects of ageing.

231 Baker Street
London NW1 6XE
Tel: 01-486 8211

Family Welfare Association
Counselling service, publishes leaflets.

501-5 Kingsland Road
London E8 4AU
Tel: 01-241 1580

GLAD (Greater London Association for the Disabled)
For enquiries and leaflets. Branches throughout London.

336 Brixton Road
London SW9 7AA
Tel: 01-274 0107

National Council for Carers and their Elderly Dependents
Advice, literature and local support groups for carers.

29 Chilworth Mews
London W2 3RG
Tel: 01-724 7776

RADAR (Royal Association for Disability and Rehabilitation)
Advice, information and publications.

25 Mortimer Street
London W1N 8AB
Tel: 01-637 5400

Counselling/psychotherapy

MIND *Address on page 151*

Women's Therapy Centres
*Counselling and workshops on
sexuality and compulsive eating.*

Birmingham	*Leeds*	*London*
43 Ladywood	Oxford Chambers	6 Manor Gardens
Middle Way	Oxford Place	London N7 6LA
Birmingham	Leeds LS1 3AX	Tel: 01-263 6200
B16 8HA	Tel: 0532 455 725	
Tel: 021-455 8677		

Divorce and separation

Gingerbread
*Local groups for one-parent families,
advice and information.*

33 Wellington Street
London WC2E 7BN
Tel: 240 0953

**National Council for the Divorced and
Separated**
*Social activities and holiday scheme.
Counselling service in several regions,
operates a postal advisory service.*

13 High Street
Little Shelford
Cambridge CB2 5ES
(day)
Tel: 01-300 4669
(evening)
Tel: 01-254 2080
Tel: 01-223 1007

National Council for One-Parent Families
Advice and literature.

255 Kentish Town Rd.
London NW5 2LX
Tel: 01-267 1361

Education

Centre for Policy on Ageing
Research and publications on older people.

25-31 Ironmonger Row
London EC1V 3QP
Tel: 01-253 1787

National Extension College
Wide range of correspondence and home study courses.

18 Brooklands Avenue
Cambridge CB2 2HW
Tel: 0223 63465

Open University
Degree level or short-term courses. Write for details of regional offices.

Walton Hall
Milton Keynes
Bucks MK7 6AA
Tel: 0908 653791

Oral History Society
Information on life history projects.

Dept of Sociology
University of Essex
Colchester CO4 3SQ
Tel: 0206 862286

University of the Third Age (U3A)
National network of branches offering study courses.

6 Parkside Gardens
London SW19 5EY
Tel: 01-947 0401

Workers Educational Association
Runs weekend courses and residential summer schools in the UK and abroad.

9 Upper Berkeley St
London W1H 8BY
Tel: 01-402 5608

Employment

Executive Stand-By (South) Ltd
Placement agency for jobs in industry and commerce. Offices also in Northwich and Bristol.

51 London Wool Exchange
Brushfield Street
London E1 6HB
Tel: 01-247 5693

Part-time Careers
For people with clerical skills up to the age of 62.

10 Golden Square
London W1R 3AF
Tel: 01 437 3103

Reach
Agency for finding work in voluntary organisations.

89 Southwark Street
London SE1 OHD
Tel: 01-928 0452

Senior Service Bureau
For people with clerical or trade skills.
No age limit.

50 Tufton Street
London SW1 000
Tel: 01-222 2289

Success After Sixty
For messenger jobs and those requiring
secretarial and accountancy skills. Fees
charged to employers only.

40-41 Old Bond Street
London W1X 3AF
Tel: 01-629 0672

33 George Street
Croydon CRO 1LB
Tel: 01-680 0858

Volunteer Centre
Central source of advice on voluntary
work and bureaux.

29 Lower King's Rd.
Berkhampstead
Hertfordshire
HP4 2AB
Tel: 04427 73311

Friendship agencies

Old Friends
Introduction service for people
over 40.

18a Highbury New Pk.
Highbury
London N5 2DB
Tel: 01 226 5432

Older Lesbian Network
Contact point for older lesbians to
apply in writing.

33A Seven Sisters Rd.
London N7 6AX
Tel: 359 7371

Lesbian Line

Address on page 157

Alcohol Concern
Information and resource centre for
local services and self-help groups.

305 Grays Inn Road
London WC1X 8QF
Tel: 01-833 3471

Alzheimer's Disease Society

Address on page 145

Arthritis Care
Information and advice on benefits
and holidays for disabled people

6 Grosvenor Crescent
London SW1X 7ER
Tel: 01-235 0902

Back Pain Association
Promotes exchange between doctors
and osteopaths. For leaflets and local
groups send SAE.

31-33 Park Road
Teddington
Middx TW11 OAB
Tel: 01-977 5474

Back Shop
Information and products for back
pain sufferers.

24 New Cavendish St
London W1M 7LH
Tel: 01-935 9120

British Deaf Association
Information, local societies and
services. Also runs courses and
holidays.

38 Victoria Place
Carlisle
Cumbria CA1 1HU
Tel: 0228 48844

British Naturopathic and Osteopathic
Association
For list of members.

6 Netherhall Gardens
London NW3 000
Tel: 01-435 8728

British Osteopathic Association
For medically qualified practitioners
and details about clinics.

8-10 Boston Place
London NW1 6QH
Tel: 01-262 5250/1128

British T'ai Chi Chaun Association
For information and instruction in
Yang style.

7 Upper Wimpole St
London W1M 7TD
Tel: 01-935 8444

Chest, Heart and Stroke Association

Address on page 145

College of Health
Promotes self-care through self-help
groups, proper use of NHS and
alternative therapies.

18 Victoria Park Sq.
London E2 9PF
Tel: 01-980 6263

General Council of Osteopaths
For list of registered osteopaths.

1-4 Suffolk Street
London SW1Y 4HG
Tel:01-839 2060

Iyenga Yoga Institute
Information on classes and qualified teachers.

223 Randolph Avenue
London W9 1NL
Tel: 01-624 3080

MIND (National Association for Mental Health)
For local MIND groups, information and private therapy centres.
Associations also in Scotland, Northern Ireland and Wales.

22 Harley Street
London W1N 2OE
Tel: 01-637 0741

Bookshop:4th Floor
24-32 Stephenson Way
London NW1 2HD

Relaxation for Living
For details about relaxation classes, tapes and leaflets, send SAE.

29 Burwood Park Rd.
Walton-on-Thames
Surrey KT12 5LH
Tel: 0932 227826

Royal National Institute for the Deaf
Technical, social and library services; also displays environmental aids.

105 Gower Street
London WC1E 6AH
Tel: 01-387 8033

Society of Chiropodists
Information on foot care and of state registered chiropodists.

53 Welbeck Street
London W1M 7HE
Tel: 01-486 3381
(2-4pm Tues & Thurs)

Women's Health Information Centre
Contact with self-help groups. Library and leaflets available by post.

52 Featherstone St
London EC1Y 8RT
Tel: 01-251 6580

Women's League of Health and Beauty
For list of classes and booklet of exercises for older women.

Rms 29-31
18 Charing Cross Rd.
London WC2H OHR
Tel: 01-240 8456

Women's National Cancer Control Campaign
Information on cervical and breast screening. Mobile clinics.

1 South Audley Street
London W1Y 5DQ
Tel: 01-499 7532

Yoga for Health Foundation
For list of local clubs and publications.

Ickwell Bury
Northill
Nr Biggleswade
Bedfordshire
SG18 9ES
Tel: 076 727271

Holidays

British Trust for Conservation Volunteers
Arranges volunteer holidays.

36 St Mary's Street
Wallingford
Oxfordshire
OX1O OEV
Tel: 0491 39766

**British University Accommodation
Consortium**
*For information on university
holidays.*

Box 184
University Park
Nottingham
NG7 2RD

**Camping Club of Great Britain and
Northern Ireland**
*Membership includes lists and maps
for access to sites in the UK.*

11 Lower Grosvenor
Place
London SW1 OEY
Tel: 01-828 1012

County-wide Holidays Association
*For walking and other activity
holidays in the UK and Europe.*

Birch Heys
Cromwell Range
Manchester M14 6HU
Tel: 061-225 1000

Holiday Fellowship
*Organises hobby and special-interest
holidays in Britain and abroad.*

142 Great North Way
London NW4 1EG
Tel: 01-203 3381

Holimarine
Self-catering holidays for the over 50's.

PO Box 2, Bilston
West Midlands
WV14 9LD
Tel: 09073 77235

SAGA Holidays plc
*Specialises in holidays for people
over-60.*

Bouverie House
Middleburg Square
Folkestone
Kent CT20 1AZ
Tel: 0303 47000

Scottish Preservation Projects
Offers training for volunteers for day and weekend projects.

70 Maine Street
Doune
Perth FK16 6BW
Tel: 0786 841479

Legal and welfare rights

CPAG (Child Poverty Action Group)
Information and advice, advocacy service dealing with welfare rights and appeals procedures.

4th Floor
1-5 Bath Street
London EC1V 9QV
Tel: 01-253 3406

Cruse

Address on page 145

Rights of Women

Address on page 158

National Association for Widows

Address on page 145

Marriage guidance

Association of Marriage Enrichment
Offers weekend courses for couples.

Westminster Pastoral
Foundation
23 Kensington Square
London W8 5HN
Tel: 01-937 6956

Association of Sexual and Marital Therapists
For list of local therapists.

PO Box 62 Sheffield
Yorkshire S10 3TS
Tel: 0742 30391

National Marriage Guidance Council
Counselling about personal relationships. For local branches see your phone book under M.

Herbert Gray College
Little Church Street
Rugby, Warwickshire
CV21 3AP
Tel: 0788 73241

Nurses support

Counselling Help and Advice Together
Literature and counselling for nurses.

Royal College of
Nursing
20 Cavendish Square
London W1M OAB
Tel: 01-409 3333

Occupational pensions

Company Pensions Information Centre
Information service.

7 Old Park Lane
London W1Y 3LJ
Tel: 01-493 4757

Consumers Association
*Reports on pensions in its magazines
and books.*

PO Box 44
Hertford SG14 1SH
Tel: 0992 59031

Occupational Pensions Advisory Service
*Resource centre for advising on
individual cases.*

327 Aviation House
129 Kingsway
London WC2B 6NN
Tel: 01-405 6922
ext. 205

Pensioners support

**Age Concern England/Greater
London/Northern Ireland
/Scotland/Wales**

Addresses on page 13

Choice Publications Ltd
Publishes *Choice* and *Yours*. Runs
retirement information bureau.

12 Bedford Row
London WC1R 4DU
Tel: 01-404 4320

DHSS
*For details about receiving your
pension while living abroad.*

Overseas Branch
Newcastle upon Tyne
NE98 1YX

**Greater London Association for Pre-
retirement**
*Provides training for professionals and
courses, publishes booklets.*

St Margaret Pattens
Eastcheap
London EC3M 1HS
Tel: 01-623 6630

Help the Aged
Raises funds for day centres,
minibuses, housing repair schemes.
Comprehensive publications list.

St James's Walk
London EC1R OBE
Tel: 01-253 0253

National Federation of Old Age
Pension Associations
Publish *Pensioners' Voice.*

Melling House
91 Preston New Road
Blackburn
Lancs BBN 6BD
Tel: 0245 52606

Pensioners Link
Groups in London for welfare rights
advice and practical help.

19 Balfe Street
London N12 9EB
Tel: 01-278 5501

Standing Conference of Ethnic Minority
Senior Citizens
Campaigns for improvement of
services for ethnic minority groups.

5 Westminster Bridge
Road
London SE1 7XW
Tel: 01-928 8108/0095

Pre-retirement

Legal and General Assurance Society
Offers a range of pre-retirement
courses.

Grosvenor House
125 High Street
Croydon CR9 3UA
Tel: 01-681 5177

Pre-Retirement Association
Advice and information on pre-
retirement planning including courses
and local groups.

19 Undine Street
Tooting
London SW17 8PP
Tel: 01-767 3225

Residential and nursing care

Central Council for Jewish Social Services
Umbrella organisation for national
network of social services, residential
and nursing care.

212 Golders Green Rd
London NW11 9DW
Tel: 01-458 3282

Counsel and Care for the Elderly
Information on private and voluntary
residential care.

131 Middlesex Street
London E1 7JF
Tel: 01-621 1624

GRACE (Goulds Residential Advisory
Centre for the Elderly)
  *Information on private homes in
  southern England.*

PO Box 71
Cobham
Surrey KT11 2JR
Tel: 0932 62928

Registered Nursing Homes Association
  *Information on registered nursing
  homes.*

74 Portland Place
London W1N 4AN
Tel:01-631 1524

Sexual therapy

Family Planning Association
  *Advice on contraception and sexual
  therapy. See your phone book under F.*

27-35 Mortimer Street
London W1N 7RJ
Tel: 01-636 7866

Redwood Women's Training Association

Address on page 144

Sports

SAGA Holidays plc

Address on page 153

Sports Council
  *Funds local initiatives, including some
  arts and craft courses.*

16 Upper Woburn Pl
London WC1H OQP
Tel: 01-388 1277

Scotland
1 St Colme Street
Edinburgh EH1 3SA
Tel: 031-225 8411

Women's organisations

A Woman's Place
  *Resource centre for women's
  information and local groups.*

Hungerford House
VictoriaEmbankment
London WC2
Tel: 01-836 6081

Fawcett Library
  *Principal UK resource for women's
  history and studies.*

City of London Poly
Old Castle Street
London E1 7NT
Tel: 01-283 1030
ext. 570

Fawcett Society
Campaigns for equality between the sexes..

46 Harleyford Road
London SE11 5AY
Tel: 01-587 1287

Federation of Women's Institutes of Northern Ireland
Provides facilities for leisure interests.

209-211 Upper
Lisburn Road
Belfast BT10 OLL
Tel: 0232 665506

Feminist Library
Principal resource for feminist information.

c/o A Woman's Place
Hungerford house
London WC2 000
Tel: 01-930 1715
(Wed to Sat)

Lesbian Line
Telephone advice and information.

c/o BM 1514
London WC1N 3XX
Tel: 01-251 6911

Mother's Union
Promotes Christianity in marriage and family life.

24 Tufton Street
London SW1P 3RB
Tel: 01-222 5533/4/5

National Federation of Women's Institutes
Crafts and cultural activities for country-based women.

39 Eccleston Street
London SW1W 9NT
Tel: 01-730 7212

National Women's Register
Nationwide network of groups for discussion and social activities.

245 Warwick Rd
Solihull
West Midlands
B92 7AH
Tel: 021-706 1101

National Union of Townswomen's Guilds
Promotes the principles of good citizenship and provides facilities for leisure interests.

75 Harborne Road
Edgbaston
Birmingham
B15 3DA
Tel: 021-455 6868

Older Feminist Network
Feminist group for the older woman.

c/o A Woman's Place
Address on page 156

Older Lesbian Network *Address on page 149*

Rights of Women
  For legal advice.

52/54 Featherstone St
London EC1Y 8RT
Tel: 01-251 6577

Scottish Women's Rural Institute
  Crafts and cultural activities for
  country-based women.

42 Herlot Row
Edinburgh
EH3 6ES
Tel: 031-0225 1724

300 Group
  Campaigning for more women in
  Parliament and in public life.

9 Poland Street
London W1V 3DG
Tel: 01-734 3457

Wesley House Women's Centre
  Meeting place for women's groups.

4 Wild Court
London WC2 B5A
Tel: 01-430 1076

OTHER PUBLICATIONS FROM AGE CONCERN
ENGLAND

■ Housing Options for Older People –
David Bookbinder

Whether you plan to move or stay put, you may well be giving some thought to the sort of housing that will suit you best. This book sets out to consider all the options open to retired people, whether tenants or home-owners, including special housing. Also covered are: financial help with improvements or repairs, home income plans, and how to get special mortgages.

Have you considered all your housing options?

£2.50 ISBN 0-86242-055-5

■ Know Your Medicines – *Pat Blair*

A guide to the medicines commonly used by older people. This handbook explains how your body works and how it is affected by medicines, either bought 'off the shelf' or prescribed by a doctor.

"I recommend it to everybody" says Dr. Mike Smith, radio doctor on the Jimmy Young Programme.

£3.75 ISBN 0-86242-043-1

■ Eating Well on a Budget

Do you love cooking fine food, but are put off by the high costs involved in preparing those delicious meals? That was how pensioners Frank and Doris Brand felt before the BBC Food and Drink Programme asked top chef Michael Quinn to prepare a week of gourmet meals with their food budget of £25. Here are the recipes, with lots of simple tips that can make all the difference to ordinary, inexpensive food.

Includes a section on nutritious eating.

£1.50 ISBN 0-86242-053-9

■ Survival Guide for Widows – *June Hemer and Ann Stanyer*

Becoming a widow can be the most isolating experience in a woman's life. This book has been written for widows, members of their families, and friends who need information about the practical and financial aspects of widowhood, as well as help understanding and coping with grief.

Written with the help of Cruse and the National Association of Widows.

£3.50 ISBN 0-86242-049-0

■ The 36 Hour Day – *Nancy L. Mace and Peter Robins MD*

Greatly welcomed by those who struggle with the frustrations involved in caring for a loved one stricken by Alzheimer's disease, related dementing illnesses and memory loss in later life, this comprehensive guide combines practical advice with specific examples. The medical, legal, financial and emotional aspects of caring at home are covered. Published jointly with Hodder and Stoughton.

£6.95 ISBN 0-34037-012-2

These books are available from bookshops or direct (post free) from Age Concern England. Please send a cheque/P.O. with order to:

The Marketing Department
Age Concern England
60 Pitcairn Road
Mitcham
Surrey CR4 3LL
